Hardship with Happiness

Hardship with Happiness

ARNOLD HARRISON

❦ **Arndor Books** ❧

First published in 2004 by
Arndor Books, 279 Manchester Road West
Little Hulton, Salford
M38 9XH

ISBN 0 9546629 0 3 *paperback*

Produced by Freelance Publishing Services, Brinscall, Lancs
www.freelancepublishingservices.co.uk
Printed in Great Britain by Antony Rowe Ltd, Eastbourne

Contents

Acknowledgements

I would like to give sincere thanks to the *Bolton Evening News* for their involvement in this book, for providing the majority of photographs and for their interest, encouragement and advice from the original concept: they provided the spark.

About the author

I am a Boltonian, having never ventured far from my roots. The call to seek greener pastures was always denied by my loyalty to the 'Town in the Bowl'. As a child in the war years the shortages, the darkness of the air raid shelters, the bombs that fell and my own futile wishes will always be remembered. As I grew and developed it was always with hardship, but with happiness, I may add, that carried me forward.

I was educated at Brandwood Street School, White Bank School and Bolton Junior Technical College and was a longstanding member of the Bolton YMCA, all to be followed by a lifetime of working in Bolton's textile industry, interrupted for a few years as 'mine host' in various hostelries in Leigh and Bolton.

On my retirement, never having had enough time previously, I turned my hand to writing and poetry and have been fortunate in having over 50 poems published in the *Bolton Evening News*, also works in many books and magazines, the most successful as a spotlight poet in the publication The Passing of Time.

I have been married to my wife Doreen for over three decades and have a daughter, two granddaughters, a great grandaughter and a great grandson, so life is never dull.

Arnold Harrison

1

Home

I was born on the first of January 1933 in Glen Avenue, Bolton, Lancashire – a day of the year on which your birthday should rarely, or never, be forgotten. Over the years this has proved so. The only down side is, however, that your Christmas present is usually described as a special one to include your birthday.

Our house was on the side of the avenue nearer to town and had a flight of stone steps leading from the front gate, steeply inclined to the front door. The garden was small but we had a wrought iron gate which was painted black to match the ornate iron railings on top of the garden wall. After the outbreak of the Second World War, the Council removed the gate and the railings together with those of our neighbours to be used for the war effort. My Mum and Dad were told at the time that one day, after we had been victorious, these would be replaced – they both went to the grave still waiting in anticipation.

Just inside the front door a small vestibule led into the front room or parlour, as my Aunty Wright would call it (my mother's elder sister, who lived with us – her Christian name was actually Georgina, which was the name of a street near to the street where they had been born, Sloane Street, Daubhill). The room was very sparsely furnished with a small sideboard and a two-seater couch. A small peg-rug lay in front of the fireplace, which I think was referred to as a Bungalow Range, from Mason's Fireplaces, Moor Lane, Bolton.

The back room or living room was much smaller as much of the space was taken up by the stairs. The room's main focal point was the cast iron fireplace with hob and oven that gleamed and shone with regular polishing and blackleading, together with the fender and the chromium-plated brush and pan set. On a cold winter's evening when the fire was drawing, the flames would sparkle and dance over the polished, black-leaded surfaces.

Built onto the back of the living room was a small kitchen which was Mother's domain. The sink with its cold water tap was under the window that overlooked the back yard. The cooker was a small gas ring, about six inches in diameter, connected to a length of black rubber pipe that came out of the wall. A meat safe with its metal grille perched in the corner on a stand. The kitchen was dominated by a large pair of wooden mangles with the 'dolly tub' and the 'posser' standing adjacent.

How Mother managed to prepare food, cook, do the washing and keep the household ticking over from such a small space I do not know. On washing day, however, it was my job to wring out the washing by turning the mangle for her – I can picture it now with splinters breaking off the wooden rollers through wear and tear and the grooves cut into them by the clothing over the years.

The back door opened into a small, flag-covered yard, at the bottom of which stood the outside toilet. Part and parcel of this small structure was the 'ash pit'. The toilet itself was a 'tippler', the operation and mechanics of which I will not delve into, only to say that this area of our kingdom was a breeding ground for vermin and disease.

On a dark winter's night, when I had to visit the little house at the bottom of the yard, I was always warned to be very careful by my mother and she would explain the perils of the tippler.

The upper floor of the house was plain and basically furnished, but always clean. A small back bedroom overlooked Shearer's pig and poultry farm, where I would stand for many an hour watching the activities taking place. Next to this bedroom was a small bathroom (alas without inside toilet) and at the front a large bedroom, partitioned into two halves, completed the upper floor.

As a six-year-old child my whole world centred around Glen Avenue and the adjoining streets; Greenhill Avenue, Greenbank Road, Willows Lane, Lenora Street and Pengwern Avenue. I knew every cobble, every gas lamp and every grid, especially the ones I had seen my marbles disappearing down. We were very lucky as also on our doorstep were Haslam Park, Willow's Lane Park and Deane Clough.

The entrance to Deane Clough from Junction Road.

There were several local shops in the area where I would be sent on errands by my Mother, and also at the request of neighbours, and these I would visit with anticipation. Each shop had its own personality, from its proprietor to its displays of goods with the aromas of fresh foods, herbs and spices.

Mr and Mrs Alcock had the 'Outdoor Licence' on the corner of Willows Lane and Bushel Street. I entered with jug in hand, the doorbell would ring and if the shop was empty one of them would appear from the back of the premises and I would hand over the jug. It would then be filled to the top with best bitter, the top of which would be a foaming froth running down the outside of the jug. I would hand over the coppers from my pocket and, clutching the jug in both hands, exit the shop for home. I was never tempted to taste the contents, having been threatened with punishment on various occasions.

However, when I was sent to the grocer's shop on the corner of Willows Lane and Greenhill Avenue, that was another matter – one of the items on the shopping list was always a warm, fresh crusty loaf which I would nibble all the corners off on my way home. The other item would be a quarter of chopped ham which I would also sample – on arriving home I would stand in the kitchen and deny all accusations made by Mother as to the condition of the loaf without corners and the slices of chopped ham with pieces missing. But after all I was a growing boy.

The local shop in Glen Avenue was an Aladdin's cave during the war years. Mother would send me every week. My instructions were always the same, on entering the shop if it was other than empty I should stand at the back and in a young, gentlemanly way allow all adults to go before me until it was empty. Sometimes this would prove to be quite a wait. The proprietor, Mr Higham, would ask me what I required which would be half a pound of butter, sugar or tea. Everything was the same price, ten shillings, which was a large amount of money at the time. He would produce it from under the counter, already wrapped up in plain brown paper and off I would go, hiding it under my jumper.

Father would never eat margarine and as we had a Bull Terrier named Dusty who would only eat butter, what was good enough for the dog was good enough for him. After the war, one day I heard my Mother say that Mr Higham had sold the corner shop, moved to Blackpool and bought a boarding house – Father referred to it as the benefits of supply and demand.

My Mother and Aunty 'Wright' had both been born in Sloane Street, next door to the mission, where I would often frequent.

Grandfather was a local coal merchant with a horse and cart that he would trundle round the streets of Daubhill. I remember well riding with him on the cart to the coal yard, which was at the back of the Stag's Head public house at Daubhill Station. There was a branch line that forked off the main line to an

Dusty the dog.

Daubhill Station, Bolton, 1965, the engine waiting to cross St Helens Road to continue its journey.

area where the coal was stocked. It was always exciting to watch the train after its delivery of coal, crossing over the main road at the rail crossing to rejoin the line and continue its journey into Bolton.

From my earliest recollections of Grandmother I can only remember her as a lady with striking white hair who because she was infirm lived downstairs in the front room. Her bed stood by the window, where she could observe passing neighbours.

Mother as a young girl of twelve years of age went to school for four days a week and worked the other day in a cotton mill. After leaving school at the age of fourteen she had been trained for a lifetime of work in the cotton mills of Bolton, and she had worked in many different mills.

I was often told stories about her life in the mills and the times she would walk to work and walk home again, just to save the tram fare – at the time it was never considered a sacrifice, but walking to places as far away as Swan Lane Spinning Co. or Canon's Spinning Co. was an act of love and necessity. The stories

Stanley Mills, Bolton, with Emmanuel Church in the foreground. Mother worked at Stanley Mills.

of her exploits as a 'card tenter', ribbon and derby tenter', 'comber tenter', 'box tenter' and 'jack frame tenter', together with some of the male workforce, such as the 'stripper and grinder', 'lap carrier', 'under carder' and 'blowing room major' all made compulsive listening as a youngster.

My father from a physical point was a large man, with a chest of forty-seven inches with everything else in proportion and he was fair-haired and strong. He would practise every day in the back yard with two fifty-six pound weights, the type that were carried on coal wagons. He would grasp one in either hand and raise one arm aloft, arm fully extended. This routine was carried out for about twenty minutes using alternate arms. On completion of his routine, which was after a hard day's work, it was into the kitchen to fill the sink for his wash – Mother would scrub his back with the brush after a generous application of Fairy Soap, then leaving him to

dry himself while she would put the finishing touches
to his tea before placing it on the table.

In his early childhood years he had lived on a farm
in Harwood and was no stranger to hard work. However, from my first recollections and for many years
after he was a motor mechanic and worked at the
Hulton Motor Company at Four Lane Ends where
now stands on the same site the petrol station next
to the Hulton Arms public house. In those days the
business was privately owned and the manager (his
boss) was Mr Vic Jones, who was also the Secretary
of Swinton Rugby League Club, and a very handy
person to know if you followed the code (Cup Tickets). The garage later changed hands and became part
of British Road Services. Wagons on the way down
from Scotland with deliveries bound for London
would stop overnight to break their journey. Bed and
breakfast was available at one or two houses off
Newbrook Road. The drivers would park their ve-
hicles in a compound at the back of the garage for
safekeeping. On such occasions it was usual for Father and his workmates to stay behind after work on
some pretence until the coast was clear, to find out
what was in the load destined for London.

One night, I think it was in 1940, Father came home
late with two large boxes of eggs, much to Mother's
delight! As it was now wartime I had never seen an
egg since the outbreak, only the powdered variety.
The following morning Father went off to work as
usual, but very soon after his departure returned
home again to tell Mother to get rid of all the eggs.

The driver, on returning to the garage for the collection of his vehicle, had discovered it had been tam-
pered with and therefore rang the Police. To remove
the evidence, Mother spent all the rest of the day
baking cakes and making custards. The kitchen

looked like Hampson's Confectioners on a busy day. That teatime I was given and told to eat twelve fried eggs. As a growing boy it was no problem, and each one was relished with the thought that it would be the last one for a long time.

Father worked for the Hulton Motor Company and British Road Services for many years, being promoted to head mechanic and assistant manager before leaving later in his life to join the staff of Fred Snaylam and Sons, one of Bolton's major hauliers.

Because Mother, Father and Aunty Wright worked I was what is now known as a latchkey child. On arriving home from school I would let myself into the house with the back door key that was hidden behind the downspout in the yard. The first job was to light the fire so that the house would be warm when they all came home from work. The previous night's fire first had to be raked out and all the ashes put into the ash pit at the bottom of the yard. I would then find paper and get the axe from under the kitchen sink and chop up any pieces of wood that I could find. After placing the paper and wood in the fireplace with a few small pieces of coal on top, the fire would be lit. Sometimes if I was cold or in a hurry I would stand the shovel in front of the fire and place a newspaper in front of it to create an updraught and the fire would soon be roaring. This had to be done very carefully as the paper sometimes would catch fire, resulting in also the chimney catching fire. It was a common sight to see someone's chimney on fire with the showers of sparks bellowing into the sky.

All the houses in our row had an ash pit at the bottom of the yard with an ornate cast-iron door in the back street wall. On ash pit day the men would arrive with the wagon and shovels (not a black bin bag in sight). Their only protection was a piece of cloth covering the mouth. The cast-iron door was removed and the ashes shovelled out onto the wagon. The pits themselves were breeding grounds for rats and as Shearer's pig farm was close by I don't suppose that helped, but I saw many rats killed with a swing of the dustman's shovel: they were multi-skilled in those days!

One of my other main chores was every Sunday morning to gather all the shoes and clogs in the house – Mother's, Father's, Aunty Wright's and my own – brown, black and suede, place newspaper on the kitchen floor and start cleaning. We had a large wooden box that contained all the equipment needed; polishing brushes, buffing brushes and wire brushes – and I was never to forget to put polish on the under instep of the shoe or it would have to be done again!

This was now the early war years and all food was scarce; Mother had to scratch and scrape and queue for hours to obtain our rations. There was a black market in ration coupons for food, clothing and toffee which could be exchanged or bought as part of daily life. At mealtimes all food served up had to be eaten, and nothing left as this was a crime. We did get to eat meat but this would always have a generous amount of fat with it, which I hated. Its taste in my mouth was revolting and my stomach would churn with waves of sickness – but it had to be eaten. During my meals I would cut it off and leave it to last, hoping that in some magic way it would disappear, but it never did. I would pick up enough courage to place a piece into my mouth, pretend to cough, take out my handkerchief and transfer it from my mouth and into my pocket. This ploy was successful sometimes but not always, and at these times it would end in conflict. Mother was very sympathetic and would try to help, but in the end Father was in charge. At the end of the meal any fat which I had refused to eat and left on my plate would be taken away and presented back to me the following mealtime. This may have been dinner, tea or the following day's breakfast. If I wanted to eat the meal the cold congealed fat had to be eaten first. More conflict would arise and I would be sent upstairs to sit on the edge of the bed and shed my own tears in private.

In those childhood days of the late 1930s and the early 1940s we had four distinctive seasons in the year, with winters very cold and with deep snow which would last for many weeks – with the first fall of winter's snow I would be out with the hand shovel to clear the steps at the front of the house and our own stretch of pavement. On completion I would survey our neighbours on either side and clear theirs as well. On completing these I would clear the houses adjoining them on either side and usually finish completely exhausted having cleared about ten to twelve houses.

I was often rewarded with a piece of cake, a jam butty, or a penny. One winter I attempted to clear the whole of the avenue but never made it, giving in to chapped hands and legs and an aching back.

On those cold biting winter days life did become more bearable as Father made me a 'winter warmer'. This consisted of an empty one pound treacle tin full of holes which had been punched in with a nail, stuffed solid with cotton waste which Mother had brought home from the mill. You lit the cotton waste and replaced the lid. Being tightly packed, the waste would not produce a flame, but smoulder slowly, producing heat. You held the tin in your hands and from time to time would blow through the holes to keep the heat generating – this was outside central heating at very low cost.

One cold frosty Christmas morning I woke up in a dark glow cast by the blackout curtains and on taking them down revealed the pale green stippled walls that even seemed cold in summer. My stocking was hanging on the corner of the bedroom fireplace (no fire). However, on occasion, when retiring at night Father would bring up what was left of the kitchen fire on the shovel and put it into the small grate of the cast-iron fireplace with a couple of coal eggs or half a coal brick. This was appreciated as much as any present that I may receive. I emptied the stocking onto the bed after straightening the woollen blanket and the various coats that had been put there to keep me warm – it was as usual, one apple, one orange and a small sack of gold-wrapped chocolate money. My big present would be waiting for me downstairs. Would it be a train set? No chance. Would it be a Meccano set? Same chance. Would it be a second-hand two-wheel bicycle? Now I really was affected by the cold.

The first job was to get dressed and take the chamber pot down and also Mother and Father's. On arriving downstairs I found Mother busily preparing breakfast after which I was given my big present. It was a large wooden fort, comparable to Disney's Magic Castle of today. The fort was detailed with several turrets, flag poles and a drawbridge, small painted wooden blocks represented various internal buildings, and it was garrisoned with a full company of lead soldiers. This was a masterpiece from Dad's shed.

Dad built his shed in the late 1930s with my help. Originally we had a small garden in the back yard which had been created by the removal of two to three stone flags. The only living plant was a lilac tree which would be about ten feet in height and every year produce masses of sweet perfumed blossom. Certain neighbours would be given a bunch, cut by Mother and delicately arranged, which I would deliver. On most occasions I would be rewarded with a penny or a very welcome jam butty, and sometimes a bunch of roses from their own garden as a treat for Mother. One day Father announced that he was buying a motor cycle combination and that he would have to build a shed to garage it. The shed would also be useful for his other hobbies and interests and become a much-needed workshop. The sad news was that the garden would have to go, including the tree. Mother and I shed a few tears. How could something so beautiful be thrown away to die? The shed occupied the space from the kitchen to the outside toilet by the back gate. It was an elaborate structure with double doors and two windows. A length of wooden guttering ran along the front with a downspout at the end for disposal of rainwater. The inside consisted of a wooden floor and a workbench, complete with a small vice at the kitchen wall end – at the other end by the toilet the coal was stored, leaving just enough room between for his combination. On the back wall of the shed was hung a large skin of dri-ped oak leather for the repairing of shoes. All his tools and equipment sat on the bench in their allotted places. There was a last for men's shoes and one for ladies' with various leather knives, rasps, tins of small brass nails and bobbins of waxed sewing thread. Under the bench was an old Singer sewing machine which had paid for itself time and time over.

The many shelves around the walls held an assortment of jam jars, treacle tins and tobacco tins, all filled with nuts and bolts, screws and washers, sagging under the weight of many more tools stacked on them. I think most of the tools had been collected over the years from pawnbrokers' shops and retired tradesmen he knew, in some cases for the price of a few pints of beer.

He would spend most of his spare time repairing shoes, making and repairing belts, purses, spectacle cases, and even repairing braces. Leather working was not his trade. He had developed his skills through trial and error and necessity.

In wintertime I think I had the best sledge in the whole of Bolton. It was handcrafted, designed and built by Dad, its runners being aerodynamically shaped by his 'spoke shave'. The seat and all cross pieces were made from tongue and groove timber, which was then woodstained and finished with a coat of varnish. I traversed the slopes of Deane Clough, Haslam Park and the adjoining fields with my faithful sledge. We were a team that searched endlessly for new and exciting thrills.

One of the many air raid shelters erected in the gardens and back-yards of Bolton in 1939.

The coldest of winter's days or nights never halted the production from Dad's shed. A Primus stove would be lit and placed on the bench to provide the meagre amount of heat and light that was needed for his work to continue.

During the war some of the houses in Glen Avenue had a post in their gardens with a small coloured board on top. This would change colour if there was mustard gas present in the air and we would apply our gas masks immediately – as a family we would sit in the house with them on, practising for any real event. There were two large air raid shelters on the back field behind Glen Avenue, one at the top and the other at the bottom. During an air raid these shelters would be full with our neighbours and ourselves, apart from Aunty Wright who, being extremely frightened on these occasions, would sit under the stairs in the kitchen and pray like the rest of us. A number of bombs were dropped on Bolton and you never forget the hair-raising shrill sound as they fell in their flights of destruction. There was also a shel-

Windsor Theatre, Bolton, popular for the double seats on the back row of the stalls.

ter in Lenora Street and one in Riley Avenue, which we also would frequent. ('If only those shelters could have talked after the War', people later said.)

Mother told me that the posh people had Anderson Shelters in their own gardens, but Dad believed the principle that, 'If it was your time – no matter the place – you went'.

In Riley Avenue lived a medium and one night Mother paid her a visit and took me along with her. At the time she may have not been able to get someone to look after me. We walked up the darkened back street, past the shelters to this house – I must have been six or seven years of age at the time. We knocked and entered the house which was full of people and in semi-darkness. I had to stand at the back of the room for the duration of the proceedings. I remember periods of quietness broken by chants and screams, followed by the shaking of bodies and the 'Amens'. That night, Count Dracula may have been playing at the Windsor Cinema but this was more scary! At the close of the evening my little legs could not get me home quick enough, but when they did, and the bolt had been closed on the back door, I was safe. This is where I lived – I was home.

2

Brandwood Street School

My first day at school was in 1938 and it still re-
mains a vivid memory after sixty-five years. I was
washed by Mother and dressed in my finery, given a
sweet and led by the hand out of the front door. Our
journey led us up Greenhill Avenue, on to Willows
Lane and I was gently coaxed all the way to the
school. Mother guided me through the large entrance
gates into the school. A few words were exchanged
with a teacher, I was given a kiss and Mother left
me with a wave of the hand. I was alone, surrounded
by hundreds of strangers.

On command we all marched in line, two abreast,
up a large flight of stairs to the next floor. Our names
were checked and ticked off before being taken to
our respective classrooms. After what seemed like
an eternity I wanted to go home and informed the
teacher of my wishes, only to be told to sit quiet and
all would be well. After a period of restlessness I
asked to leave the room, which I was allowed to do,
at the same time given directions to find the toilet.
I never did find it in time, the result being a personal
accident, which also produced floods of tears. I was
lost, I was abandoned, I was wet through and I was
going home! My escape from school went unchal-
lenged and I easily found my way home. Although in
tears I was happy standing on the front doorstep

knocking on the door – Mother welcomed me with open arms, asked me what was wrong, dried my tears, washed and changed me and dragged me back to start again.

Brandwood Street School is still a landmark in Bolton and can be seen from any high vantage point round the town. It was only a short walk from home to school and I would cut through Willow's Lane Park and enter the playground by climbing over the back gates of the school which were always locked.

The games we played at breaktime were 'Kick Out the Ball', 'Finger-Thumb-or-Icky', hopscotch, pitching bottle tops against a wall, and marbles. It is sad to think that all these magical pastimes are now gone forever. To have a full bag of marbles or a full pocket of bottle tops would bring you instant fame and following.

At the start of the war a large underground air raid shelter was built in the park which was adjacent to the school and once a week we had evacuation practice. The school was evacuated as quickly as possible and all pupils marched over to the park and taken underground. I remember those dimly-lit passages as we were guided to our allotted area and seated down on wooden forms. The air was always damp and puddles of water would have to be negotiated in reaching our places. Naked lights at various distances along the passages provided an eerie illumination. After hearing the 'all clear siren', it was organised chaos in getting out – puddles would be ignored in the race to the surface and daylight.

One of my best friends who lived in Lenora Street had a much older brother, who took us both one night to the park to help him. I realised later in life that he broke into the shelters and, with a torch taken from his pocket, led us to his destination, which was a large

Ardwick Street, Bolton, after a wartime air raid.

bank of batteries that provided the power to illuminate the shelter. He dismantled these, found a plank of wood and we carried them all out two or three at a time. We staggered down Willows Lane to his house in Lenora Street and stacked them all in the back yard. The most amazing thing was that we made four or five journeys back and forth, with no person stopping us or enquiring as to our behaviour.

As children the greatest attraction in the park was the open-air swimming pool, which in summer was a hive of activity. This was located in the far corner of the park by the side of the playground. On a hot summer day if you arrived late at the park the pool would be full and you would queue at the entrance gate hoping for an early admission. This was not always possible and you would go away disappointed.

The noise of other children playing and the splashing of water made you vow that tomorrow you would be earlier.

In winter the pool was still an attraction, although officially closed. Access was gained by climbing over the railings. We would slide and skate over its frozen surface in our clogs, all falls and bumps being completely ignored. The winters were much more severe then and the ice would form much thicker and last longer than the present day.

Whatever the time of the year an eye always had to be kept open for the park keeper, Mr Popplewell, who lived in the park house facing Hawthorne Road – his son Granville was one of our gang but this carried little favour in any transgressions.

One day on arriving at school we were all informed that even as children we could help the war effort by having a paper-collecting week, items to be collected being newspapers, books, magazines and comics. We were to approach our parents, neighbours and local shops and all collections were to be brought into school and deposited in a special area provided. A few days later I brought my own collection in and was excited to see a large bundle of comics tied up with a piece of string, already donated. I myself did not get the *Dandy* or *Beano* and only read them on the odd occasion through the generosity of a pal. The temptation was far too great. I picked them up, had a quick look at them, checked that the coast was clear and stuffed the bundles up my jumper. Where could I hide them until school finished in the afternoon? The answer came in a flash. The boys' toilets were outside in the playground and would make an ideal hiding place. I furtively made my way out of the school and went into the toilets after checking that they were empty. I chose the end cubicle for a quick getaway, stood on the bowl and hid them behind the cold water cistern.

For the rest of the day in school I was on pins, sure

that my guilt-ridden face would lead to discovery. But no, I was in the clear!

When school was finally finished for the day I held back in the playground until all had gone home before picking up enough courage to look for my spoils. The bundle was still there waiting for me, and I eagerly grabbed it and hid it beneath my jumper before making a quick exit over the back gate of the school. I ran all the way home and on entering the house was able to evade Mother in taking them upstairs to my bedroom. Later in the evening after tea, I was feeling safe and sound in the sanctuary of the bedroom with all the comics spread over the bed, when Dad walked in and the game was up. I was explained the error of my ways, but given forty-eight hours to read them all before taking them back to school. Dads were wonderful after all!

The pleasure of reading though was tremendously enhanced by the installation of electric light which replaced our previous gas lighting. I can still picture the shadows dancing and flickering on the walls and ceiling and hear the constant hissing of the gas. Going to bed at night up a darkened staircase to a cold room with visions of these dancing shadows always brought a chill to my body and raised the odd palpitation.

In those early childhood schooldays, spending money was non-existent, but I did have a weekly treat. Each week, it was either Monday or Tuesday night, I would go to Melbourne Road Church situated on the corner of Willows Lane. The price of admission was twopence and you also received a drink! The superstar attraction was 'Felix the Cat' with all his black and white adventures. It was always packed. We were always noisy. It was a ball. Felix was the king long before Elvis. The projector on occasion would break down – so what? He would soon be back with his magical tricks before finally disappearing into a black dot in the centre of the screen. When the show was finished, we left knowing that it would be another week before our return, but the sadness would soon be forgotten especially if one of us had a penny hidden in the depth of his trouser pocket. Facing the church on Willows Lane was a chip shop, which incidentally is still a chip shop over sixty years later. For one penny (there were then of course 240 in the pound) you could purchase a 'penny mix'. Every coin you had in your pocket then was valuable and had purchasing power – unlike the present day. The penny mix consisted of a few chips, a piece of broken fish, a few peas, finished off with a sprinkling of scraps, all doused in salt and vinegar.

During life at Brandwood Street School a great amount of our spare time in lunch breaks and after school was spent on the park playing cricket, and frequently someone would hit the ball over the trees onto the bowling green. The irate bowlers would summon Mr Popplewell, the park keeper, who in turn would chase us off. His son Granville may have been playing with us, but this still carried no favour. The park also had a playground next to the swimming pool, with slide, see-saw, swings, monkey frame and wedding cake.

The land at the far side of the park was open and wild, leading down to the brickworks which was between Deane Church Lane and St Helens Road, covering a large area. It always seemed to have a hypnotic attraction for children – I think it was the brick kilns which we would go into when no one was about, of course those not in use. They were warm inside and covered in layers of dust. A tunnel ran from the brickworks, under Deane Church Lane to where we called the 'shale hole' which was a large pit filled with water on the open land at the rear of what used to be Hulton Lane Isolation Hospital. Through this tunnel ran a railway line on which small wagons travelled. They were used to carry some type of waste from the brickworks to be dumped into the 'shale hole'. When trespassing on the brickfield an eye was kept open for any adults, but if all was clear we would climb over the gate at the entrance to the tunnel and walk under Deane Church Lane to the far end. We were in the bowels of the earth. This was real adventure – would we encounter Flash Gordon and the Claymen?

When I finally left Brandwood Street School to further my education, it was with great sadness and trepidation. One thing that I missed – no more putting pieces of 'carbide' into the inkwells and creating 'mini-volcanoes' on the desks leaving teachers with the uncertainty of their chosen vocation!

3

Deane Clough

As children much of our outdoor life was spent in Deane Clough, getting dirty, getting wet and getting into trouble. If we had to pay a call of nature there was a gents' toilet situated by the side of the church on the very edge of the ravine. Who had designed and built it I do not know, only that it was in a very precarious position. It was common practice to use

Deane Church, Bolton, 1928: standing on the edge of the Clough, it is magnificent to behold.

the toilet as quickly as possible and get out as it pro-
jected a vision of oneself ending up in the bottom of
the Clough clutching a piece of paper. A short distance away was a cave halfway up the side of the
Clough, which we believed led into a tunnel that ran
all the way to the Town Hall in Bolton. As it was
during the war we thought the reason for this was to
provide an escape route to safety for all the powers
that be in case the town was invaded. One Saturday
morning, we all arrived at the Clough with an assortment of spades, picks, shovels and garden imple-
ments to dig our way through the cave and find this
tunnel. This adventure was not longlasting as we
were chased away and told to go home and never return.

As you entered the Clough from Junction Road and
walked down its deep slope, on the left hand side were
terraces of greenhouses and allotments which were
carefully and lovingly tended by their owners in the
cultivation of vegetables. On the right hand side of
the Clough was 'Pickies Field' in one corner of which
was a small pond. In summer it was alive with newts
and dragonflies, which would skim over the water
evading every attempt to be caught. In desperation I
would throw my coat as a net, but without success.
We had been told that if you caught one and took it
to the chemist on the corner of Deane Church Lane,
they would give you sixpence. For all the time that I
wasted, if I had ever been successful, the price should
have been the 'Town Hall Clock'!

In the field grew what we called 'hay nuts'. This
was a tall plant with a white flower.

We would find a stick or a piece of twig and dig
these up revealing a small bulb or tuber which we
would wash in the stream that ran down the Clough
and then eat.

My recollections are that they were crunchy, sweet and tasty. Over the years I still have not discovered what we ate, but I am happy with the fact that they must have been harmless. If we were thirsty it was also common practice to drink from the same stream that ran down the Clough (not advisable in the present day).

I became a member of the 1st Deane Bolton Cubs and most of our activities were concentrated in the Clough; camping out, building bridges, woodcraft skills and nature studies. As a cub, my duty on Deane Sermon's Day was to stand with a collecting box at the bottom of the path that ran from the rear of Deane Church down to the Clough. During the day I would go back to the church two or three times to empty the box of its contents and marvel at the sight of the cascading halfpennies, pennies, brass threepenny pieces, silver threepenny pieces and sometimes a sixpence. Deane Sermon's Day was always widely attended as a day for families to be united and the community to worship together in celebration.

Doffcocker Lodge, Bolton – the Lodge provided many a fish for Mother's pan!

The Clough was the starting point for many adventures. We would travel the length of the Middle Brook from the first bridge to the Iron Bridge at Beumont Road, which during the war was a camp for soldiers. Along the full length of the road on both sides were parked hundreds of tanks in preparation for any impending invasion. Sometimes on a Saturday we would be more adventurous and on reaching the second bridge, climb the steps on to Ladybridge Lane which brought us to Chorley New Road, before crossing to wend our way up Markland Hill to Doffcocker Lodge. After watching the fishermen for a short time, we would continue our journey up Old Kiln Lane to 'Bob Smithy' and tramp the length of Walker Fold Road to the valley. We would spend time running backwards and forwards through the round brick tunnel which carried the stream to Barrow Bridge, before following the stream through the valley onto the moor. We would

Walker Fold, Bolton, 1930, a short walk from Barrow Bridge and the sixty-three steps.

*Scotsman's Stump, 1938, erected in memory of George Henderson, a
lonely traveller who was murdered.*

again dally on our journey, climbing the odd tree and
searching the moor for wildlife before finally arriving
at Scotsman's Stump. We would read its history and
ponder its significance before continuing. On reaching the end of the moor a rest would be taken on a
form situated overlooking Belmont Road and the
Wright's Arms public house. On the side of the hill
nearby was an army pillbox, a concrete structure and
gun emplacement. The hillside would be searched for
any spent ammunition – if you did have such items or
a piece of shrapnel, that was street cred of yesteryear
and priceless. From there it was only a short walk (all
downhill) to the Wright's Arms and a bus into Bolton
and eventually home to Deane: many miles of walking, exercise and fresh air on a couple of sandwiches
in a brown paper bag and a bottle of water. Now I
think I would need a tank of 'lead free'! Deane Clough
was our adventure land where we would do battle with
the Germans and become a hero.

The Middlebrook, Bolton, home of the stickleback and the elusive Red Doctor. The tower of St Saviour's Church is visible in the distance.

The stream that ran down the Clough flowed into the Middle Brook where I began my fishing exploits as a boy. I would spend hour after hour travelling its length in anticipation. My equipment was a straight pin that was bent to form a hook and a piece of the finest string I could find, tied onto the end of a stick. My keepnet was a jam jar borrowed from one of the graves in Deane Churchyard. My bait was a worm and my quarry the stickleback. I know quite well why they are so called having had my fingers punctured on several occasions. The pangs of hunger and wet feet did not deter the quest for the elusive Red Doctor of that species. Any fish caught were put into the jar and carried home with both hands. Other boys would be shown: they could look, but not touch.

I gradually progressed to the One Hundred Foot Lodge down by the side of the Iron Bridge on Beumont Road. Originally it had been a stone quarry and was quite dangerous, being very deep with dark forbidding water. It was popular, however, as a swimming hole although only the bravest of boys would jump off its highest rock to disappear below its dark surfaces. After fishing this water and catching the odd fish or two and at the same time on several occasions almost falling, I decided that it was not the ideal place because of the swimming and diving activities.

Because of my interest, Dad started fishing himself. I supposed, to rekindle his boyhood days and to support me. But no! We were now fishing as a team and fishing for the pan. His motorbike combination carried us far and wide. The sidecar filled up with all our equipment, including food and drink and me perched on the back. Traffic on the roads was almost non-existent and I will always remember the crack of the exhaust on an early Sunday morning. His favourite place was Doffcocker Lodge which was only a short ride from home. We would chug up Markland Hill in the fresh morning air and park at the top on the main road. Our gear would be unloaded and carried along the path leading us on to the lodge. This water was always popular and we would carefully pick our way past all the other anglers to a vacant place and set up our shop.

Right from day one, Dad instilled into me that when we fished it was with worms, and only for perch! Any other fish was of no interest or use. Any perch caught weighing about half a pound or over went home for food. I became a dab hand in the kitchen, cutting off the head and tail, removing the dorsal fin, gutting and cleaning, dusting with flour and putting into a frying pan. It was the days of necessity and self-preservation and, take it from me, they taste very good. Not quite in the same class as silver hake, but they very pleasantly satisfied one's hunger.

One morning we had caught about six small fish which we had put into the keepnet, to be released before going home, not being big enough for the pan, when Dad asked me to go to the bike for something, and off I went. As I was gently stepping my way along the bank, so as not as to disturb the other fishermen, I came acros someone who my young eyes thought was an old man and enquired as to how he was doing. 'Just caught the one' was his reply, 'How about you?'

In my eagerness to impress I blurted out 'Six. I have caught six.'

He looked at me, at the same time pulling his keepnet to the edge of the water. 'Six indeed. But are they as big as this?' I looked and thought I was seeing what I can now describe as an ancestor of Jaws. He explained that his type of fishing was known as 'ledgering' on the bottom. He did not catch many, but when he did, 'Look out'. I could not imagine anywhere in the world a frying pan big enough for that type of fishing.

Dad and I visited many waters in and around Bolton, ponds, lodges, reservoirs and private waters included – sometimes with permission, other times not. On the occasions we were approached by a water bailiff the exchange of a shilling worked wonders. Mother always waited for our return with the greatest anticipation and we seldom let her down.

Getting up early on a Sunday morning to visit waters new was always worthwhile. Just sitting there on the basket, all my attention firmly fixed on the top of the float, which would sometimes be hidden by flashes of sunlight or the ripple of the water, all thoughts of school, rationing and German war planes would be gone into oblivion. I was at peace, my only thought being how many would I catch for the pan!

4

White Bank School

My next school after Brandwood Street was White Bank, which originally had been a large mansion situated in Haslam Park. The owners had donated it to the town and in turn it was converted into a school. The ground floor classrooms were the original morning rooms and drawing rooms with large bay windows and ornate fireplaces, the only addition being the rows of desks which had been installed.

Haslam Park, Bolton, 1929, where White Bank School was situated.

Long before I attended, the grapevine had warned us about the perils and discipline which awaited us. In the mornings, all the school assembled outside in front of the school. The entrance was up a flight of stone steps, the top one of which had been 'dolly-stoned' a gleaming white. Mr Morris stood at one side of the entrance, cane in hand, with eyes fixed firmly on the top step. On command all pupils entered the school in single file. Anyone who had the audacity, or accidentally put a foot on the top step, was dragged out of the line and whacked. The reason given was that a cleaner had spent time and effort on her hands and knees for our benefit and their work had to be appreciated.

The school's most famous teacher was Mr Jess Morris, a king of the classroom, a legend in his own right. To see him in one of his lighter moments entertaining the class by dressing up as a Chinaman in full costume and makeup and reciting 'The Man Who Only Had One Hair' was never to be forgotten. On the other hand in his classroom was a large wooden cupboard containing a wide selection of canes, long ones, short ones, thick ones, thin ones, flexible ones and rigid ones – all waiting for you to take your pick – you had choices.

As new boys we were informed that we had come to school to learn and this would be achieved the easy way or the hard way. But in the end, we had to learn and reach a standard. To learn the easy way was acceptable, but to learn the hard way would require a few adjustments. During one morning's lesson he stood up from his desk and informed us that he had to leave the room and would be back in five minutes. We were to carry on with our work with no misbehaving. After about ten minutes, no Mr Morris had appeared and certain boys had started talking and walking about the room. I myself sat on the back row of desks with a large bay window behind me. I was asked by one of the boys to go and join him and at the same moment had an impulse to turn round slowly and look behind me. There to my horror was Mr Morris, standing in the bushes, looking into the classroom, with a piece of paper in one hand and a pencil in the other. He was writing down the names of those running rampant. With the revelation that I had seen him, he put his finger to his lips, telling me to keep stum! A few minutes later the classroom door partly opened and he pretended to be speaking to someone for a few seconds before actually entering. This of course gave time for one and all to return to their desks. The room was now silent as he stood before us, coughed and produced his piece of paper from his pocket – all of the names that he called out were invited to join him at the front of the class and asked to take their pick. It was usually three strokes on each hand. We were new boys, and were only caught once. It never happened again – we got the picture. After that he could have left the room for the best part of the day, knowing that all would be in order.

The following day during class, the door opened suddenly and the father of one of the boys came into the room and made straight for Mr Morris who was sitting at his desk. 'Yesterday you caned my son who came home crying', was his outburst. 'And I am going to report you.'

Mr Morris stood up from behind the desk, rose to his full height and replied, 'This is private property. You are trespassing and if you do not leave these premises at once I will have you evicted and furthermore if you ever address me again in this manner I will cane you as well.'

The boy's father spluttered, turned about and left the room, the confrontation over.

On one occasion, I myself strayed from the path to break the rules and received six strokes on each hand. I arrived home crying and in a sorry state. My Father enquired why, and I told him. He took me into the front room, sat me down on the couch and began to educate me. He was my Father and when at home it was his job to teach me and punish me for doing wrong. But when at school the teacher was paid a wage to teach me and also to punish me for doing wrong. In the future if I was ever caned at school on arriving home he would cane me also. After thinking about this, there and then I decided to go to school and behave, do as I was told and on no account get the cane.

Every Tuesday morning Mr Morris would choose two boys to go out for his lunch. This was an honour and also you had time out of school. One Tuesday I was chosen with another boy and given the money for his two pies and off we went. After walking to the top of Melbourne Road our destination was a confectioner's shop on Willows Lane where we purchased his beloved pies. After leaving the shop with the bag clutched in my hand, we began to argue and act the goat and the inevitable happened: the bag was accidentally knocked out of my grasp and the pies sent rolling down Melbourne Road, which is very steep. When they finally came to rest, on examination, we found them to be broken, dirty and contaminated. The feeling was sheer panic. The way to salvation would have been to go back to the shop and start again. The only problem with that was that we did not have a penny between us. I wiped the pies with my handkerchief and removed the black pieces from the crust. But they still looked like candidates for the nearest pig bin. My so-called school pal refused to come back with me and went home.

On arriving back at school, I sat awhile on the park wall gathering courage before my forthcoming confrontation. I knocked on the classroom door before entering, to see Mr Morris sitting at his desk, feet up, with a look of hunger on his face. He was alone. Everyone else had gone. 'Arnold where have you been – where is my dinner?' I could not speak and just handed him the bag, waiting for the explosion. He calmly asked me for an explanation, which I gave him in detail. He explained the errors of my ways and thanked me for being a man in facing my responsibilities. The following day when my so-called friend who had deserted me returned to class, the cupboard was opened and he was asked to select his choices.

It had been a happy ending for myself, but never again was I asked to be a 'pie boy'.

It was a warm summer's afternoon and I was absent from school. I had declared a holiday after what had been a disastrous morning at the hands of my teachers. I was in the park, on my own and at peace with myself, sitting on the grass. I had chosen to sit on the top of the hill which overlooked a stream that ran through the park. On the other side of the stream was the main railway line that ran in and out of town. I had prolonged the consequences of my actions, but all the same had torn out a page from the back of one of my books to record all the names and numbers of the trains that would pass before me during my afternoon of leisure. When a train approached from the distance its rhythmic emission of sound and its plume of black smoke would be heard and seen long before any visual contact. As it came closer and into view the noise intensified with the clouds of smoke obscuring the train from view. People however could still be seen at by the windows looking out, and on occasion one would wave to the young stranger on the top of the hill. I myself would wave in return as thanks for their recognition, and ponder who were these people riding on this train, where did they live, were they going on holiday, and if so, where? All questions and no answers.

On the other side of the railway line was a very large cemetery whose far perimeter edged on to open moorland that carried to the horizon. The vista before me was viewed with trepidation as the plumes of black smoke seemed to mingle with the gravestones and then weave their way across the wild moorland. A man with a small dog was passing close by and I decided to ask him for the time. He observed me for a few seconds before telling his dog to sit and then produced a shiny gold watch out of his waistcoat pocket and conveyed the time to me in a loud voice. It was as though I should not have been there, or why had I the audacity to break his peaceful concentration? I had plenty of time to pass before going home to an empty house. My only chore was to light the fire and get the house warm. As it was the season for conkers I decided to raid the horse chestnut trees in the cemetery, which I had done on previous occasions. I jumped to my feet, picking up my bag at the same time, and carefully placed my list of train numbers behind one of my book covers for safe-keeping. The railway line and stream were crossed by a stone bridge which had a cobbled surface leading to a dirt path on the far side. The path led up a steep hill to the cemetery gates which, due to being exposed to the elements over the years, were deeply rutted and difficult to climb.

On entering the cemetery, without hesitation I made for the horse chestnut trees, and found to my dismay that the trees had been stripped apart from a few on the very top which were beyond my reach. Not all was lost, as I already had a varied selection at home, stored in the bottom of my wardrobe, all which had been soaked in vinegar and in different stages of hardening, waiting for the day they would be used in combat. As it was near the perimeter fence of the cemetery my eyes were drawn to the open moorland before me that gradually climbed to the distant horizon. On various occasions other boys and myself had ventured over the fence and onto the moor, but never far. There always seemed a reason for us to turn back to the safety of our known environment. I felt strange as wisps of smoke beckoned me to follow. I renewed the grip on my bag and stepped onto the springy surface of the moor before me. There were no paths. But this was no hindrance as it was an open view which gently flowed into the distance. As I walked into the unknown, the air was still; all sound had been turned off. No animal or bird life, no faint sound of a distant train, all these no longer existed or were part of life. It was like walking on the surface of a giant painting, the horizon being the top of the canvas.

The nature of the moor began to change and become very rocky. I now had to pick my way round large boulders that stood before me – on passing the final boulder that was obstructing me, I found myself on the top of a ridge, where a valley lay before me and civilisation.

A row of about ten stone cottages nestled on the side of the valley, which I made for with haste. Where was I? Would I be able to obtain a drink of water, as I was now thirsty? How far was I away from home?

All were questions that needed to be answered. As I approached the nearest cottage I again felt the same stillness in the air and a strangeness. The front door on which I gently knocked was slightly ajar, and after waiting several moments I decided to enter, calling out as I did. The room was small, but cosy. A two-seater couch, brown in colour, faced a stone fireplace, the mantelpiece of which was adorned with small ornaments and expensive-looking trinkets. Many pictures decorated the walls – some landscape, some portraits, but mostly pictures of cats. I left the room through an open doorway, which led to a small kitchen, the centrepiece of which was a large wooden table. The table itself was set with bone-handled cutlery and expensive china. Various stone jars and their contents stood on the top of an old dresser together with silver-framed pictures of yet more cats. There were pots and pans on the draining board of the sink, and a long-handled broom was leaning against the back door. In the far corner of the room a steep narrow flight of stairs led to the upper floor which I climbed with caution. What was waiting for me and what would I find? I was not disappointed. For in one small bedroom I found a large money box bursting with two-shilling pieces and half crowns which I greedily stuffed into my pockets.

In the other bedroom on a small but elegant dressing table lay rings, necklaces and other jewels which I examined and transferred to eagerly awaiting pockets. I came downstairs excited by what I had found and departed by the front door to explore the rest of the cottages in the row. They were all the same, empty and full of treasures. By this time my pockets were full, but I had no hesitation in discarding all my books from my bag and using it to carry more treasures. Again my head was filled with questions without answers. Where was I? Had I walked into another time? Where had all the people gone? And why? Everything I had seen was from many decades past. I decided it was time to make my way home, so with bag in hand I reluctantly left the last cottage, to find that outside all was covered in a black fog. It must have been the smoke that had woven its way over the moorland.

Which was the right direction home?

I chose my direction and began to fight my way through the blackness. As I struggled, I faintly heard a sound that broke the stillness. As the sound grew stronger it formed words that penetrated my mind with a devastating realisation. 'Wake up Arnold. I am still waiting for the answer.'

'Yes, Mr Morris. What was the question?'

The cane I chose was short and not too heavy, the theory being that it may not be wielded with the same power as a longer one. I was wrong!

Mr Morris of course was not the only teacher at White Bank and we did not learn by being beaten into submission. But I was never caned again. Our other teachers were just as dedicated and outstanding but not looked upon with quite the same reverence. I can still picture Mr Tong and Mr Mayoh, their footsteps echoing over the highly polished wooden floor as they would hurry from classroom to classroom.

Once you had entered the school through the main doorway, you found yourself in the main hall of the house. An ornate magnificent staircase stood before you, leading to the upper floors. At the foot of the stairs stood a large marble sculpture of a Greek god or a Roman hero with a body of perfection, its only adornment being a fig leaf that was placed in a strategic position. We were told as new boys that when autumn arrived and the chill of the forthcoming winter was in the air, the leaf would fall. During the depths of winter it would draw furtive glances from time to time.

After many happy years at the school, and countless exploits – a story in itself – I passed the examination to attend Bolton Junior Technical College and left with great sadness. Ex-White Bank pupils from all corners of the earth will agree in saying that it was not easy, but fair. You learned respect and tolerance and that common sense goes a long way.

5

Helping Out

Mother and Father worked hard and saved their coppers. Every chance I had, I would contribute to the pot and longed for the day I would start work and be able to help more. Little did I think at the time that work would last for fifty years.

In 1942, as a nine-year-old boy, on Sunday morning after doing my chores and having breakfast, I would walk from my home in Glen Avenue to Daubhill Station to start my morning paper round. My employer was a very large rotund man who had great difficulty in walking. All my papers would be bagged and waiting for me. My round was the full length of Deane Church Lane, including many sidestreets running off. My wages for the round were 1s 6d (7½p).

The week before Christmas I had a very good morning. Almost every household I delivered to gave me a tip. Besides delivering their papers I had to collect the money for them, which on completion was given to my employer, who by the way had told me that because it was Christmas I was on double wages, 3s (15p). This thought filled me with elation all through my work.

When I finally reached the other end of the lane in Deane, my jacket and trouser pockets full of money, he was waiting for me with the news that his other boy, who did his next round, had not turned up and would I do the extra round? As it happened I knew his round as previously I had walked round with him for company and to help; it covered Kirkebrok Road, Hulton Lane and onto the estate, Chip Hill and Towers Avenue. I would also get 3s (15p) for doing his round.

When I eventually finished, tired and weary, he was waiting for me on the lane with one of his paper bags spread out on the pavement. I was instructed to empty all my pockets onto this, which I did: mountains of shiny copper and silver, half crowns, florins, pennies, ship halfpennies, brass threepenny bits, silver threepenny bits, tanners. He gave me 6s (30p) and told me to go home and he would see me the following Sunday. I looked at all the money lying before me and asked him about all the tips I had been given. He informed me that it was his paper business, I was only the paper boy, I had been paid my wages and all the rest was his. On arriving home late for my dinner clutching 6s in my hand, which I gave to Mother, I told my Dad of my fortune and misfortune. The following Sunday my dad would not let me go but went himself to Daubhill Station. I don't know what was said but he came back with 5s (25p) for me, and that was the end of my paper delivering.

My next Sunday morning endeavour to earn money was to deliver milk from the Co-op building then at the junction of Willows Lane and Deane Church Lane. Early in the morning a lorry would come with the crates of milk from the depot in Bolton and leave them stacked on the pavement, by the gable end of the building on Willows Lane. I was usually early and had to wait for my employer who was called John. This particular morning I waited for about an hour without a sign of him. One of the customers, a lady, had decided to come and investigate why she had not received her morning milk. I told her that I was waiting for John but as she was here, to take her own milk.

I realised that people must be waiting and decided to do the round myself. The procedure was to climb over the double metal gates into the back yard of the Co-op, go inside the shed where a wooden handcart was kept, take a key off a hook in the shed, unlock the gates and wheel out the handcart before finally relocking the gates. I stacked up the cart with crates and off I went.

I clattered round the adjoining streets; Lenora, Glen, Pengwern, Annis, Bushell and many others. In general people were glad to see me as I gave them their milk and collected the empties, apart from one or two who were waiting for the first cup of tea of the day. I returned to the Co-op to refill the cart with still no sign of John, and off I went again. I was happy, I was singing. Would this be my line of work when I grew up? I was on my own, out in the fresh air, no one to boss me, providing a service: I was at peace with the world.

I had almost completed the round when I noticed a man walking down the street towards me waving his arms and shouting 'Who are you?' and asking what I was doing with the Co-op handcart. I explained that I worked for John and got 2s (10p) a week. He hit the roof and informed me that I was too young and should not be working and to get off home. I parked the cart at the side of the road and turned away to leave. He then realised that he was left holding the baby and stopped me. As I had nearly finished the round, he asked, would I please continue and he would see me back at the Co-op, stressing that I must be very careful and take my time. When I did return, John had turned up and was receiving a dressing-down. Strong words were exchanged and John was sacked on the spot.

It seemed that the day before he had gone on a men's picnic to Blackpool and had been left behind, somewhat the worse for wear. His boss thanked me for my toil, gave me 5s and that my services would be no longer required.

I was not having a lot of luck with my efforts to provide money for the pot. My next venture was with a friend of mine at Deane Golf Club as young caddies. This was a job I really enjoyed. I was young and fit and could carry the bag as good as well as anyone. Although I did not know a three wood from a nine iron I would just offer them the bag and let them choose.

I walked up and down those green fairways, up and down the hills with enjoyment. I could see trains (especially namers) coming out and going into Bolton. At the bottom of the golf course by the side of Deane Clough was a windmill which you could hear groaning and squeaking as the arms rotated. The only down side to the job of being a caddy was that on arrival at the club you had to wait in a shed until chosen by one of the gentlemen golfers. They would enter the shed, cast an eye on the labour available, and choose. It was like a Miss World contest: you smiled and looked intelligent.

It was the war years, the time of self-preservation. Every little helped. Every day the fire had to be lit at home and I needed wood. My foraging took me all over Haslam Park, up and down Deane Clough, up and down the Middle Brook, over the back field, and even to 'New York' (end of Junction Road). Everything was in short supply and on ration. One task I hated the most and caused me the greatest embarrassment. I was given a paper bag by my Dad and off I went. I would start at the bottom of Hawthorn Road, walking up the roadside gutter to Hulton Lane, then crossing over, returning along the gutter back to Hawthorn Road, all the time looking for and collecting spent cigarette ends. I was like a golfer keeping my eye on the ground, hoping no one would recognise me. When I arrived back home Dad would put a piece of newspaper on the kitchen table and empty out this bag. He would take out his penknife, cut them open and sort out all the particles of tobacco which were put into a tin to be smoked later in his best briar pipe.

A few years later my next adventure to help out with the family finances was as a programme-seller for Bolton Wanderers. This was the most rewarding and pleasurable use of my time so far. I had started to watch the Wanderers a few years earlier and remember my heroes well. The names of Atkinson, Banks, Butler, Eastwood, Goslin, Hanson, Heslop, Hubbick, Hunt, Sidebottom and the leader supreme – Nat Lofthouse – will be remembered forever. Later in life I read about an instance when Sam Bartram, the Charlton goalkeeper, was asked what was the most frightening experience he had ever encountered on a football field. His reply was the sight of Nat Lofthouse in the penalty area with the ball at his feet. It was 1946 and I was the age of thirteen years and an experienced programme-seller. It was that fateful day of 9 March when I left home and walked to town using all the short cuts from Deane, over Daubhill and Lever Street, across the Orlando Bridge onto Manchester Road and then to Burnden Park. I arrived a couple of hours before kick-off and collected my coupons from a building which was outside the

Burnden Park, home of the Superwhites and legends of greatness.

ground at the railway embankment end. These were put into a bag that Mother had made me and off I went to my patch by the Orlando Bridge.

Home games were always a huge attraction, and you would see the same faces and characters week after week in the throngs of supporters, happily chatting and demonstrating as they headed for Burnden. All traffic stopped. Anyone in a hurry would be advised to get out and walk.

When you had sold up, it was back for more supplies, returning as quickly as possible. At a certain time before the kick-off you had to return to the office to settle up, paying in all the monies that you had collected and receiving your wages. The best part of your remuneration was a free ticket to watch the match.

All the turnstiles had supporters queueing up and struggling to get into the ground, but with my ticket clutched in hand I gained access by being admitted through the main entrance, passing through the players' tunnel onto the track. We sat on forms in front of the Manchester Road paddock with the railings as a back rest. I remember well all the activity and movement on the railway embankment as stretchers were carried back and forth by people with painful expressions and urgent cries for help. I never realised the seriousness of the situation and what in fact was happening. A man's voice behind us screamed out, 'Get out of the way boys. We are coming over.' We all jumped up and ran onto the pitch as hundreds of supporters came over the fence from the paddock. Everyone was shouting and gesticulating, as it seemed unreal at the time and one could only wonder, 'What and why?'

Unknown to me of course, Mother and Father were at home listening to the traumatic reports being broadcast on the wireless. After the match I walked home to Deane and on entering the house was hugged and fussed over by Mother. Alas, that was the end of my programme selling days for Bolton Wanderers; Mother and Father were both in agreement.

❦ **6** ❧

Special Days

Always a favourite day out was a visit to Barrow
Bridge. Mother and Father would take me, sometimes
with Aunty Wright, to town where I would wait patiently and full of anticipation for the bus to arrive
for our journey. When we had boarded and left town,
the landmark I would be looking for was the Barrow
Bridge chimney. When I saw this I knew there was
not very far to go.

*Barrow Bridge boating lake, Bolton, with its famous chimney in the
background*

On a Bank Holiday or a summer weekend there
would be hundreds of people there, all strolling up
and down in a holiday atmosphere. As you walked
up the road from the bus terminus, noise and laughter would be heard coming from the lake. I would
run up and down that road, climbing onto the wall,
legs dangling over the stream which ran parallel to
the road. On the other side of the stream was a row
of cottages with their gardens sloping down to the
water's edge. They catered for visitors by providing
food and drink in the form of sandwiches, salads,
cakes and cream teas, all to be consumed in the open
air setting of green lawns, red roses and the singing
of birds. They were always busy and I would watch
children with their parents being served large pots
of tea with china cups and dream that one day that I
myself would be crossing the water and joining them,
but it was never to be! When I asked Mother why, I
was told that those people did not work in the mill
and that we were not as fortunate.

On arriving at the lake my thoughts would turn to
the pleasures at hand. Father would hire a rowing
boat for us, but as this was a very popular activity,
we would sometimes have to wait for one to be called
in. As an alternative you could always have a ride
round the lake on the 'big boat' as Mother called it.
At the side of the lake was a café where we would
have our refreshments. These would be sandwiches
brought from home which had been made by Mother
after breakfast, leaving us just to purchase a pot of
tea and if I was lucky a glass of Vimto for myself.

The day was never complete until we had walked
up the sixty-three steps, counting each one as we
ascended. On reaching the top we would continue
through the fields to Walker Fold, spending time
breathing the air and enjoying the vista before

The Sixty-Three Steps, Barrow Bridge, Bolton, 1933. On every visit it was mandatory that these were climbed and precisely counted.

returning back to Barrow Bridge and the bus home.

One Bank Holiday in the early 1940s was to be something special. I was to be taken to Belle Vue and I was going on the train. I had never been on a train before and the wonder and activity of Trinity Street Station held me spellbound. I was hurried down the stairs onto the platform as the train was pulling in - the smoke, the steam, the noise, clanging of doors, people scrambling into compartments. Where was I going? A blast from the guard's whistle and a wave of his flag and we were away.

On arrival in Manchester, having left the station, we seemed to walk through endless streets before boarding the bus for our final destination, Belle Vue.

Trinity Street Railway Station, Bolton, 1935. The canopy stood until 1968, and the station and buildings were demolished in 1987.

As I stood in a long queue with Mother and Father outside the entrance, I was unimpressed with its exterior. But this was soon to change once we had entered. The first main attraction that caught my attention was the incomparable 'Bob's' with the screams coming from the frightened passengers in its carriages. I was too young to be taken on 'Bob's': that experience came later in life (not very pleasant as it turned out to be). But the alternative was a ride on the scenic railway followed by braving the terrors of the ghost train. There were sideshows, amusement machines, shooting galleries, the zoo and reptile house. I was treated to a ride on an elephant – all this and on our doorstep!

There was the Belle Vue Speedway, which incorporated the rugby league ground. These pleasures I was to savour later in life together with the famous King's Hall wrestling arena. In my teens, as a wrestling fan, I would be a regular visitor to see my heroes – Anaconda, Bert Asserati, Farmer's Boy, Jack Pye, Dave Armstrong, Ernie Kiwi Kingston and many more. All under the strict supervision of referee 'Dick the Dormouse'. Sometimes as an added attraction the evening would end with a spectacular fireworks display.

Belle Vue was the Disneyland of the North and much in advance of its time, being the forerunner of all today's modern theme parks.

On reflection, I think without question my favourite childhood pleasure was visiting the New Year Fair which was held on Moor Lane. As part of my Christmas present I would be given a small amount of money and as it was my birthday the following week, on New Year's Day, a small amount for this as well. I would go on my own from Deane and walk into town, which meant more money for the fair. As you approached town the noise could be heard from the steam organs and traction engines that powered the attractions. Before leaving home I had converted all my money into small change to prevent any mishaps. I would have copper in one pocket, brass threepenny

New Year Fair, Bolton, 1935. Roll-a-Penny, Hoopla and All Press – this time the weather seems to have won!

pieces in another and sixpences in another. Any shillings or florins would be wrapped up in my handkerchief and buried away.

As you entered the fairground through one of its many entrances the atmosphere was electric, with the hustle and bustle of happy people, some clutching bags of roast potatoes, candyfloss, and in some cases coconuts that they had won. As you walked round from attraction to attraction care had to be taken in navigating the masses of cables lying on the cobbles, supplying power from the generators. After two or three circuits of the fair to breathe in its atmosphere, I would plan what I would do and where I would start. It was exciting just to stand in the crowd outside the boxing booth with the adults and watch the gladiators on show and hear the challenges

New Year Fair, Bolton, 1945: in search of pleasure after years of hardship.

being issued by their promoter. The invitation was to allcomers – the reward being £5 if you lasted three rounds, which was a large amount of money at that time. There was always someone willing to try – many with the help of Dutch courage. The fights were bloody with no quarter given, bursted noses and closed eyes being very common. There was always a big cheer for the losing challenger with cries of 'Bravo!' and 'Hard lines', but once again the £5 note stayed in the wallet. After all the excitement I was hungry and made my way to the Black Pea Saloon. On a cold winter's night this was the best place on the fair. You sat down on wooden forms in the rear of the tent, clutching your cup of peas which you had doused in vinegar. In front of you was a brightly burning brazier, the heat of which would envelop you and may cause you to linger and perhaps purchase a second cup of peas. When warm and sufficed it was back outside into the blaring noise and excitement.

The main rides I selected were always the same, the Big Wheel, the Moon Rocket and the Waltzer. The side shows round the perimeter of the fair that provided my pleasure were the coconut shys, darts, guns (shooting down ping-pong balls and breaking clay pipes), the Wall of Death, the Marvels of Nature – being the bearded lady, the five-legged sheep and the Siamese twins. Much of my well-protected money alas would be frittered away on the Roll-a-Penny. I would very gently roll my penny down the slide, aiming for the square which had the value of sixpence and watch it rolling round before slowing down, usually to come to rest on a line. I would watch with disappointment as the penny would quickly vanish into the hand of the operator. The man of the hoop-la stall would be holding an armful of rings and explaining how easy it was to the people passing by. I would try with grim determination, using dexterity of hand and eye in an attempt to encircle a new ten shilling note or a watch – but it was always 'Hard luck son – try again'. Once I explained my hard luck story to Father. How close I had been – the ten shilling note was almost mine. He told me if I ever tried again to take a two-pound hammer with me as that was the only way I was going to get the ring over.

As I remember one of the most popular attractions was the 'All Press'. People would queue and wait until a place became vacant for a chance to play. The stall was round with a wooden ledge running round its circumference, and set into this ledge and equally spaced were a series of bell pushes, each one representing a railway station and each individually named. In the centre of the stall were vertical display boards with rows of small electric lamps, each one representing a bell push and station. When all stations had been occupied it was then time for the off. A switch was activated and a light would flash in sequence from station to station. On command all players would press their pushes and all eyes would be on the flashing lights. After a couple of minutes the lights would slow down and players' fingers would turn white in an attempt to control its final destination.

When it finally stopped, that station was the winner and the prize was the pick of the stall. One night it was my turn, and maybe the operator had taken pity on me because of my age or my looks of desperation, but I was the winner. After surveying all the prizes on offer I selected a chrome-plated brush and pan companion set for Mother. This took pride of place on the hearth for years.

From time to time I would keep my eye on the Town Hall clock, taking into consideration the fact that I would be walking home as I would be skint. My last gamble would be to walk round the fairground, eyes glued to the floor, searching for any monies that some unfortunate person may have dropped. And it did pay dividends; a sixpence or a shilling would be found. This would be used in a last final fling and I would still be walking home.

The Pictures

My first memories of going to the pictures were with Mother and Father, which was to the Majestic cinema on St Helen's Road. I was young and not really interested at the time – I suppose I had to tag along as babysitters had not become fashionable. The redeeming feature of the whole evening for me was that on walking home after the show, we stopped at the chip shop on Deane Church Lane. It may have been a special anniversary or occasion because we went into the small dining room at the back of the shop and sat at one of the vacant tables there. In addition to the food that Father ordered, as extra we had bread and butter and a cup of tea. How strange that small incidentals are remembered for the rest of one's life. All through my childhood and teenage years I can never recall Mother and Father dining out anywhere other than this chip shop or the one on Wigan Road that faced the Queen Anne and Stag's Head pubs. How times have changed.

A couple of years older and the pictures had become a passion for me, and I now went to the Majestic on a Saturday on my own to join the multitudes of thrill seekers in our weekly pilgrimage. I went fully armed (today's description would be 'tooled up') with my 'Jew's Harp', spud gun and potato tommy talker and pea shooter – a 'Rambo' of yesteryear. All ready

Lido Cinema, Bolton: on a Saturday night the queue would reach outside, to the rear of the building.

to create as much noise and disturbance as possible. Our heroes of the silver screen were the weekly serials that ran forever – 'Zorro', 'Hopalong Cassidy', 'The Clutching Hand', 'The Purple Monster', 'Deadwood Dick' and 'The Skull'. Adventures and excitement that lasted for years.

If the main film of the programme was British it would be greeted with boos and derision. We were not interested in the quality of acting or the quality of the spoken word! The question was – would the plane crash? Would the stagecoach go over the edge of the cliff? Would the bomb be defused in time?

On desperate occasions to obtain money for the pictures we would climb over the back yard gate of Allcock's off licence on Willows Lane and subtract a few empty bottles out of one of the beer crates stacked in the yard. We were then stupid enough to go into the shop, put them on the counter and ask for our

Tivoli Cinema, Derby Street, Bolton, 1938, previously the old Derby Cinema.

money back. Mr Allcock would look at the bottles then look at us, giving a wry smile, before opening the till and giving us the coppers.

He knew! And he knew that we knew he knew, but played along just the same. However, on the odd occasion he would look at the bottles we had placed on the counter stating they were not his and to return them from wherever they came – we had no answer.

To my delight I then discovered the Windsor which I could easily travel to by tram, the fare being one halfpenny. This was situated in Gate Street off the left hand side of Deane Road opposite the Saviour's church. If the tram fare was not available it was an easy walk down the hill at Deane, passing the Aranda Garage and Steels provision merchants. For the local courting couples the back row downstairs consisted of double seats making the Windsor a somewhat more attractive venue.

In that era of the film industry we saw the best! Who can ever forget the three stooges, Leon Errol, Andy Clyde, Tom Mix, Boris Karvlov, Bela Lugosi and Lon Chaney Junior together with the exploits of the Bowery Boys (Leo Gorsey and Huntz Hall). William Boyd reigned supreme as Hopalong and Charles

Starret as the Durango Kid – we had Chester Morris as the romantic upholder of the law, Boston Blackie. And who would ever fail to remember the smouldering and mysterious looks of Turen Bey?

When I was earning spending money from my various part-time jobs, paper boy or milk boy, a special treat was to take in the Windsor first house, run outside when it had finished, jump on the tram and go down to the Regent for the second house.

Week after week, when coming home on the tram, you would see the same adult characters who had been into town and were one over the eight. Some would be hiding a parcel of chips and fish under their jackets, no doubt as a peace offering when arriving home. But many would be smelled out by a keen-nosed tram conductor and evicted on the spot.

By my early teens I had become a town picture-goer, mainly frequenting the Odeon, Lido and Capitol

Queens Cinema, Bolton, not the most popular in town until the showing of The Outlaw.

as the favourites but still having many choices in the town – the Theatre Royal, Queen's, Embassy, Regal, Rialto and Royal. On a Saturday night you would have to be in town very early to catch the first house and even then you may have to queue. The queues would sometimes stretch from the front of the cinema all the way outside to the rear of the building – people would still be queuing after the second house had started, knowing that they would not see the full show. As a last resort it was always easier to get into the Queen's Cinema as they did not seem to show such popular films as the rest and it was just a little further out of the town centre being at the bottom of Trinity Street, Station Brow. This image was to drastically change and improve their standing on the showing there of the most controversial film of the day, 'The Outlaw', starring Jane Russell. This film,

Rialto Picture Playhouse (Cinema), St George's Road, Bolton, was one of the first cinemas in the town to convert to Bingo.

Odeon Cinema, Bolton, 1983. The Odeon was a popular venue for Saturday tea followed by an extensive film show and a singalong on the organ.

together with Bill Hayley's 'Rock around the Clock', were both masterpieces of hype and advertising.

What also made the Odeon, Lido and Capitol the main attractions was that they all had thriving restaurants where one could obtain chips, egg, bacon, sausage, bread, butter and tea, all for about 3s (15p). Your entertainment was also superior – for the price of your ticket the show would consist of a 'B' picture (which would last over an hour), the news, next week's trailers, a cartoon or travel film, followed by the main film and if it was the Odeon, a rendering of the organ with singing in between. This was value!

At the immediate ending of the night's programme, it was customary to leap from one's seat and dash out before the playing of the national anthem: not as a gesture of disrespect but to get to the tram station for the last one home. If this was missed, it was a long walk home as taxis were a definite luxury for the well-to-do.

When in town one Saturday, just after lunchtime, with my pal Wilf we were walking past the Capitol and I noticed that the ticket office was quiet and on impulse purchased two tickets. I put them in my wallet, came out and we carried on with our tour of town. After having tea at home it was back to town to go to the Capitol. When we arrived there was the usual large queue stretched out before us. Wilf and I walked straight in and when informed that the cinema was full, stated that we were going to the gents and proceeded to go upstairs. We gave our tickets to the usherette much to her surprise, who told us that it was full and that the ticket office should not have

Theatre Royal, Bolton: also a venue for Big Band Concerts and the fabulous 'Ink Spots'.

issued them, but as they had done so and we had come upstairs we could go in and stand at the back or at the side until seats became available.

I still feel guilty, thinking of all those people standing outside in the rain and the cold. The same ploy worked many times after that.

The Theatre Royal, besides being a cinema, held Big Band concerts on a Sunday night, which were always very popular and well attended. Icons like Stan Kenton, Eric Delaney, Eddie Grey and his Band of the Day, together with many others deserved our admiration and our cries for more.

One week Mother and Father had secretly booked tickets for all of us to see the Ink Spots who at that time were at the height of their careers. This was a feather in someone's cap in bringing them to Bolton. Whoever it was should at the time have been presented with the 'Town Hall Clock'. I can still hear them singing 'Whispering Grass' – Windsor Davis and Don Estelle did a good job but you can never beat the real thing.

I know I was a picture fanatic and totally dedicated but every Monday night without failure it was the Grand Theatre on Churchgate, where I sat upstairs in the 'gods' – Monday night would set the standard for the rest of the week. Any entertainer that made it through the night would work the rest of the week, but if not it would be Bye-Bye. Even on a Monday night Churchgate would be a hive of activity with throngs of people on the move. In such a small area the choice for one's vices was unequalled in any other part of town. We had the Man and Scythe, the Brass Cat, the Bush. A short stroll away were the Bull and Wharf on Church Wharf, Smokey Joe's Temperance Bar, the Grand, the Theatre Royal, the pasty shop, and the Capitol. You gained access to the gods by the side entrance to the theatre up a flight of spiral stairs. At the top a lady in a small pay box would be waiting for your 'nine pennies'. With ticket in hand it was through the door, hoping that a decent seat would be found. The buzz of the people, the chatter and clink of the glasses in the downstairs bar, the warming-up of the orchestra led by the renowned talent of Joe Hill; we saw them all, the greatest and brightest stars of yesteryear, singers Joseph Locke (Mister X), Ronnie Hilton, Michael Holiday, Issy Bon. I don't remember Des O'Connor though! Comedians, included Frank Randle, Nat Jackley, Norman Evans over his garden

The Grand Theatre, Bolton, entertainment supreme and a palace of pleasure, sadly missed.

wall and these were a vast variety of speciality acts; Wilson-Kepple and Betty and their Dancers of the Desert, Wild West marksmen with Indian knife throwers, strongmen who would challenge you to break a six-inch nail, bend a horseshoe or rip a telephone directory in half. We even had the great Fred Parry entertaining us with his talents of table tennis – where has it all gone and why? Certainly not in the name of progress.

❈ 8 ❈

The YMCA

As a young boy and a pupil of White Bank School I joined and became a member of the Bolton YMCA. Our leader was Mr Freeman, a man of dedication to his position and a good servant to Bolton over the years. I myself spent many years of quality time at the YMCA in the presence of my fellow man. Every Tuesday and Thursday evening were for physical

Knowsley Street, Bolton, 1929, in those days a cobbled street.

training. After leaving school in the afternoon, it was home for tea, washed and changed, collect my gear and off to town. The main entrance was on Deansgate but admittance to the building was gained via the entrance in the side street adjacent to the Hen and Chicken's pub. After climbing two flights of stairs the door at the top led into the main room, and directly facing you were the changing rooms, showers and toilets.

After warming up with a few forward and backward rolls on the coconut mats, we would assemble in single file to begin a circuit of all the different pieces of apparatus. The first was the ceiling ladder, where you could perform your own version of Johnny Weismuller as you swung from arm to arm. If you fell down it was back to the start again. The next task was to climb ropes suspended from the ceiling which required concentration, strength and agility. It was then onto the parallel bars, finishing with the vaulting horse. After four or five circuits the blood would be pumping and the adrenalin flowing.

After winding down, our coach would explain our strengths and weaknesses and what to improve on before our next attendance. As it was school the following day, it would be a quick shower and home.

Sunday evenings were never to be missed. Although it was of a religious theme we would have a guest speaker with a lantern slide show, describing to us the wonders of Egypt, the jungles of Africa and the rivers of Borneo, all of which would be enthralling and stimulate the imagination. This would be followed by tea and biscuits, a game of draughts or snooker. Very simple but happy times.

In the early and mid 1940s my annual summer holiday was with the YMCA at their summer camp, 'Lakeside', on the side of Lake Windermere, a few miles up the road from Newby Bridge. The camp was very basic, the main part being a large wooden building which was the dining room and cookhouse. Each boy had daily duties to perform – peeling what seemed like thousands of potatoes, washing cooking utensils, scrubbing the long wooden tables, serving and waiting on, and general carrying and fetching. The rules were easy: no working, no food. We slept in bell tents on straw mattresses, about eight boys to a tent. If you were unfortunate enough to require the toilet during the night it was a walk into the woods to locate a large hole which had been dug for this purpose, across the centre of which was a not too wide plank of wood. You had to be very careful and have a good sense of balance. It had been known from time to time that some unfortunate boy had slipped and fallen in to you know where. What trauma and distress! They would be the talking point of the camp for the rest of the holiday and shunned especially at mealtimes.

As part of the facilities the camp had three or four rowing boats which we would use on trips across the lake and for fishing.

The highlight of the week was always a day trip to Grange-over-Sands. We had to walk from the lakeside camp all the way to Newby Bridge to board the train, which was quite a walk. Our time in Grange would be spent looking at the shops, roaming the seashore, sometimes a visit to the cinema, and spending our last coppers on sweets.

One year on our return from Grange back to camp, we arrived at Newby Bridge all tired and hungry to begin the dreaded walk before us. I knew every bend in the road; all the posh houses that I had passed many times before, wondering who was lucky enough to live in a house like that; the sawmill which stood

on the left-hand side of the road, one of the land-
marks that had to be passed before reaching camp
and please would there be any food left?

A car approached us from the rear which I am sure
was an Austin Seven and the driver asked us would
we like a lift. We explained our destination and that
there was in fact ten of us. This made no impression
on the driver who was an elderly gentleman and invited us to get on board. We managed six inside with
the driver, two clinging outside on the back and one
on each side clinging to the doorhandles. We never
saw another car on the road and all got back to camp
safe and sound – but alas there was no food until
breakfast the following day.

At the end of the war the YMCA had started to run
educational holidays in Europe. As I was still a member Mother and Father saved up to allow me to go to
the Black Forest which had been arranged with the
German Youth Hostel Association as part of the re-
unification plan. The journey started as I boarded
the coach in the town centre, bags safely stowed away.
Mother and Father said goodbye and it was off to
Folkestone. I was going to a foreign country. Time
was spent going through pockets, checking my be-
longings and counting my money and chatting excit-
edly. Very little sleep was taken on the journey before
arriving at Folkestone.

I boarded the ship, bag in one hand and documents
in the other, following the rest of the party led by Mr
Freeman. Lines were cast away and all thoughts concentrated on our destination which was Boulogne.
On arrival after passing through Customs we boarded
a local train for Paris and once there discovered that
we had to cross Paris for our next train which would
take us to Basle in Switzerland. The best way to ac-
complish this was to cross Paris on the Métro. It is a

good job that we had someone in our party who could speak French or we may have still been there. During our wait on the underground platform I had to pay a call of nature. After deliberation as to which was the Gents I went in, and there to my horror was a French woman sitting at a table, one half piled high with rolls of toilet paper and on the other half a tin box. The system was any gentleman requiring paper had to buy it from her, at so many centimes for so many sheets. From that day I have had reservations concerning the French and won't drink French wine. I don't know if there is any connection but it did have an impact. I wonder if the same system is in operation fifty-five years later.

On the train to Basle we had a sleeping compartment and awoke in the morning to the pulsating noise from the rails and the call that breakfast was being served. On all those gigantic expresses that crossed and recrossed the countries of Europe, the food was excellent. On our arrival in Basle we had a few hours to wait before our next train to Freiburg in Germany. This was spent in the Botanical and Glacier Gardens, general sightseeing, and eating and drinking. We had been across France, Switzerland, and now were to enter Germany. For our destination, Freiburg, we had to wait another few hours before our final leg to the Black Forest. This again was spent sightseeing and changing our money into German Marks. When we eventually arrived, bag in hand, tired and hungry at a large house by the side of a lake it had been thirty-five hours since leaving Bolton. The house itself belonged to the German Youth Hostel Association and during the war, the occupant had been Martin Borman who was the second-in-command to Adolf Hitler: this was Borman's Headquarters. During our stay one day I was taken into the cellars of the house and shown two large metal doors which were the entrance to a tunnel. This was a large square structure, concrete-lined with electric light fittings. A German staff car was parked there in readiness for a quick departure in case of invasion.

In the kitchen was a bread-slicing machine which was used to cut large loaves of bread. Each morning one of our party would be up early to alter this machine to cut thin slices. Later one of the Germans would be up to readjust it to cut thick slices. Just before the cook came on duty we would alter it back to thin slices. From that day and that holiday, I don't think the Germans ever forgave us. Thus the phobia on towels on sun beds developed.

Every day was spent playing table tennis under the shade of trees, fishing and developing friendships. I had taken with me as part of my luggage two jars of coffee which I gave away to new special friends. You have never seen such gratitude and genuine pleasure that those two jars of coffee created. They both wrapped them up carefully to be taken home for their own parents.

During our stay as a special treat we were taken on a two-day trip to Lake Constance. During the journey one of the meals that had been arranged for us was in a convent. We sat at long tables and were waited on by the nuns in full uniform. The meal was sparse but wholesome and filling. The beauty of the place, its history and aura made every fibre tingle. It was another world, another time, I was privileged to share.

We stayed the night in a water tower by the side of the lake and only arrived there at dusk, all travelweary and dying of hunger. The officials in charge were kind enough to organise us a quick meal before bedtime, which alas became a disaster. We were served a type of German sausage with salad. But the problem was everything was drowned in oil. I had never tasted such, and neither had anyone else in our party!

Hunger, however, compelled us to try it, but without success, and all food was returned uneaten to the disappointment of our hosts. It was empty bellies until breakfast the following day. We again beat the Germans by being first down to breakfast.

Sadly our holiday eventually came to an end and we were faced with another thirty-five hour journey back to Bolton. As always, the return journey seemed to pass quicker than the outward one, maybe because all our time was spent discussing our exploits, adventures, sights and friendship and what we had bought for our parents.

9

Our Gang

At the back of Glen Avenue was Shearer's pig farm which is now the tennis courts for St Ethelbert's School on Hawthorne Road. After the farm had been demolished and the land cleared, this was known as our back field, where our gang ruled against all invaders, especially the Brick Field Gang.

Our gang: what a motley crew – Granville Popplewell, Rene Goth, Jimmy Sharrock, Roy Marsden, Billy Alcock, Ernest Quarmby, Kenny Holehouse, Alex Theckston and myself. Names to conjure with and faces to imagine! Every day when we came home from school, a fire would be lit on the field and this was kept burning until bedtime. We played our football, marbles, top and whip, up and down the back street. For a change we would play cricket in Back Pengwern Avenue, using the gas lamp as the wicket. The number one rule was, if you hit the ball into someone's back yard, you had to go and fetch it and you were out. If there was any dispute as to being LBW you would have to carry on the innings by using the bat upside down and playing with the handle. From time to time we would be troubled by an older boy, not of our gang, who would give us grief. We played with a tennis ball and as he thought of himself as a future England centre forward, he would demand that the person holding the ball throw it into

A kerbside enactment of the Boat Race, 1936, off Spa Road, Bolton.

the air so that he could head it. One day one of us
(not me) produced an old cork ball out of his trouser
pocket and hurled it into the atmosphere. Our would-
be future England centre forward soared into the air
like a gazelle, and came down like a sack of potatoes.
We were never troubled again.

One of our gang lived on Willows Lane, and I was a
frequent visitor to his house, often being invited for
tea and the occasional party. We were playing in his
house one afternoon when there was a knock on the
front door. He opened it and we were both confronted
by a man in uniform, covered in gold braid and shiny

buttons. He identified himself as an uncle of my friend
and could he come in, explaining that he was a sub-
mariner in the Navy and on leave. My friend told
him that his mother and father were both out at work
and would not be home for some time. He came in
and made himself at home, stating that he was hungry and asked where his mother kept the ration books.
He searched the top drawer of the sideboard and took
every ration book he could find; food coupons, toffee
coupons, clothing coupons – the lot.

Books clutched in hand he was off to do some shopping at the corner shop, informing us he would return
shortly. He did return with about twenty tins of baked
beans. The navy must have turned him into an addict.

When my friend's mother and father came home, I
had already left and was out of the firing line. I never
actually found out what happened and can only sur-
mise. Did his mother blow him up? Did the Germans
blow him up? Did he blow himself up?

One of our other haunts where we would carry out
our gangland activities and continue with our make-
believe was in the pig farm. Mr and Mrs Shearer's
children sometimes invited us to play with them in
the house. They had a secret. In one small darkened
ground floor room was a wooden-hinged door in the
floor which when raised, revealed a deep well, which
we had to jump over to be in the gang. I could still go
today to those tennis courts at St Ethelbert's and pin-
point that well within two to three metres.

When they left the original farm and moved to
Junction Road I would visit them for many years after. But alas as progress marched forward that farm
became part and parcel of the reconstructed Deane
Golf Club.

As mentioned earlier, when I was a pupil at
Brandwood Street School we would put pieces of

carbide into the inkwells to create mini-volcanos: this was comparable to a washing machine over-generously filled with powder, set into motion and the door left open. Carbide itself when put into water produced a very explosive gas which burned intensely. It was used in various types of lamps to provide illumination for cars, bikes and road lamps, etc. One evening, however, we as a gang dropped a full tin down one of the water grids situated in the kerbside gutter in Glen Avenue. One and all made a quick retreat out of harm's way – a piece of paper had been previously tied round a stick which was lit and thrown towards the grid. What happened was not a mini-volcano – it was the real thing! Flames shot to the height of the rooftops and one and all were covered with a coating of stagnant sludge.

After the initial shock and the realisation of the consequences we disappeared to all points of the compass. For many months to follow our local elders blamed it on the Germans, including Mother and Father. But the question was always raised, why no apparent damage? The answer suggested was it must have been a dud – one and all kept quiet for the rest of the war.

If during the day while out playing there was an air raid warning we would run with haste to the shelters, as these were also used as our headquarters and gang hut. A piece of candle was always left hidden inside for such emergencies to provide illumination and ghost stories would be told (the setting being ideal) and as a dare to imitate our elders, pieces of paper would be rolled up tightly, one end would be lit and we would attempt to smoke (not to be recommended).

While playing on the Middlebrook in the vicinity of the Iron Bridge (Beumont Road) with much difficulty we discovered our greatest shelter of all. It was possible to climb inside the bridge and crawl inside the huge girders which were part of its main construction. We were now inside a steel cage and bomb proof – as long as the Germans did not aim for all the tanks parked above our heads and the army barracks.

In wintertime as Mother and Father would be working I had many days off school with their permission and instructions, which I would spend queuing up at the Victoria Pit which was on the site where now stands Barton Grange Garden Centre. I had a homemade trolley in the shed consisting of a wide plank of wood and four small wheels which would be pulled from, home up Wigan Road, passing Beumont Road and into the pit yard, to join a long queue, all waiting patiently. There was an assortment of

Victoria Colliery, Bolton, 1951, during the war years a supplier of the coal bricks and coal eggs that helped to make life tolerable.

trolleys, prams, sledges and anything that could carry a few coal bricks or half a bucketful of coal eggs. It was hard work but had to be done, the options unthinkable as survival depended on the family working as a team. We would always bump into someone we knew which would make the journey back home more acceptable.

As members of Deane Church and Deane Sunday School some of us were coaxed into becoming members of the 1st Deane Bolton Cubs and I was a member of Wolf Patrol. Cubs met on the top floor of the large stone building on the corner of Horsefield Street and Junction Road which overlooked the entrance to Deane Clough. You reached the top floor by climbing a dimly-lit spiral staircase which, on a dark winter's night, would play tricks with your imagination.

On Cub night I would leave the house in pristine condition, uniform ironed and starched, woggle adjusted to the right position, lanyard gleaming white, my Swiss army knife and my Madras police whistle polished to perfection. In addition, after much begging I acquired my final finishing tough to complete the image. This was a wooden staff that Mother bought for me from Albert Ward's in town. I was to spend many happy years with the troop, marching and exploring the moors of Belmont, Turton, Edgworth and Rivington. At weekends, Mother and Father hardly ever saw me.

One very memorable weekend we stayed in a hostel, which I remember as a single storey wooden building in Bradshaw by the side of the brook. As this was my first time at the hostel, we had been warned of the ceremony which we would have to go through during the weekend. After many hours of waiting and anticipation, the time finally arrived. The brook was dammed to make a small deep pool, we had to undress to our shorts and be ceremoniously ducked and re-christened with our new, born-again, chosen nick-name. To my everlasting shame, the best they came up with for myself was 'Parsnip', which stood for many years. Later in life, however, I did have a change of heart as to its significance on my development for their taste.

In summertime, on long warm evenings, we would engage in the building of various types of bridges over the stream that runs down the Clough. Our skills for the tying of knots and the lashing of timbers would be put to full use in a practical way.

In the early 1940s, as a member of Wolf Patrol, the day that was the proudest and looked forward to the most was Deane Sermons. We would all march through the churchyard, flags held aloft, to enter the stone archway into the church's magnificence.

One year I was chosen to carry the flag, which had been beyond my wildest dreams. I was young. I was fit and strong. But on the occasion I trembled. Also around the same time I was to have the honour of being given a trial to sing in the church choir. The adrenalin was at bursting point but the outcome was 'Don't call us. We will call you.'

On the day of the Sermons Deane village would be a hive of activity. All church services would be fully attended, especially the evening service in the open air of the churchyard. During the day, graves would be attended and adorned with fresh blooms, and fami-lies would stroll at leisure up and down the Clough. Even Father would attend – not as an avid church-goer – I think the attraction may have been that the village taverns had a reputation of serving suste-nance longer than their permitted hours.

My demise as a member of Wolf Patrol came about after a never-to-be-forgotten weekend attending a jamboree in the grounds of Smithill's Hall. We left our headquarters pushing a large wooden cart containing our tents and camping equipment plus food all the way to Smithill's Hall. What a journey!

The Saturday was spent pitching camp, sorting out our supplies, exploring, playing with new friends, listening to speeches of welcome, and in the evening singing our songs round a large fire. Each tent was self-sufficient and looked after itself. Our Sunday morning breakfast was, however, a complete disaster, with our burnt sausage and bacon being buried in a convenient hole in the ground. To compensate for our frustration other boys and myself decided to chop down a tree with our newly-acquired axes, which were an addition to our image. This was not appreciated by the powers-that-were at the time (it was not even close to Bonfire Night). Our axes were confiscated and were never to be carried again.

On cub night I still left the house in pristine condition, but I would leave my staff in the air raid shelter (Back Glen Avenue), run down into Wigan Road and jump on the tram to the Windsor Cinema. At the paybox I would be given enquiring glances as to my appearance but this was of no concern as I had three pennies in my hand to enter anew the world of adventure, escape and make-believe. I was no longer a gang member. I was now an individual.

10

Strutting the Town

Saturdays became a ritual of 'strutting the town'. The tram fare from Hawthorn Road to the terminus in town, which was at the back of the Wheatsheaf pub, was only one halfpenny. That was the smallest value coin in your pocket but still had great value – not like today's coinage.

From the terminus we would walk back to Great

The first railway line to serve Bolton from Great Moor Street Station to Leigh was opened on 1 August 1828.

Moor Street Railway station to savour the excitement
of the arrivals and departures of the trains. I still
feel ashamed that on some Saturdays we would stand
on the Town Hall square, explaining to passers-by
that we had lost our tram fare home and would be in
trouble, the idea being that if you collected three pennies you could go home on the train from Great Moor
Street Station to Daubhill Station, as this was the
first stop after leaving Bolton. We would then walk
along Deane Church Lane, cutting through the brickworks to get home.

After our spell of train-spotting it was on to Newport Street – pausing to look at the cakes in the window of Orth's confectioners, before carrying on to
Trinity Street by cutting through the back of the
Railway Hotel onto Trinity Street. Our destination
was the footbridge that spanned Trinity Street to
Great Moor Street. Besides being a much used short-
cut linking these two parts of town, many happy
hours were spent, again watching the trains steam-
ing in and out of the station from the raised position
of the bridge. From time to time you would get envel-
oped in clouds of smoke but this was more than com-
pensated for when you spotted a 'Namer'.

We would cross Great Moor Street in front of the
Municipal School and enter Gregory and Porrits.
Every stall would be looked at and their contents
studied, before leaving to run round the corner onto
Bradshawgate. All shop windows would be looked into
and dreams formulated with wishes expressed to each
other.

But our next destination was to be Smokey Joe's,
to sit in the back room drinking hot Vimto. We would
plan and contemplate the rest of our time in town –
would we encounter 'Jimmy Clean Clogs', would we
see 'Freddie' dressing the window at the Great North-

ern and Southern Stores, and above all would we encounter on our travels the greatest strutters of the day being 'Dominic Pye' (of the famous Pye wrestling family, led by the invincible bad boy Jackie Pey) and his associate 'Big Nick'?

When Dominic and Big Nick walked side by side along Newport Street, the pavement was full and one and all would step out of the way without hindering their progress. They could strut the streets of Bolton in safety.

After leaving Smokey Joe's we would look at all the still pictures of the film stars outside of the Theatre Royal, Capitol and the Embassy which was on the next corner by the side of Woolworths. Woolworths itself was our next call, not with the intention of buying anything (we had no money) but to mingle and look with the droves of other Boltonians who paid homage on a Saturday to its premises.

The only time I would be rewarded with a treat was in my earlier years when Mother would drag me to town to have my picture taken at Mr Fox's photographers. The treat would be for sitting still and behaving. I have penned a few verses as a reminder of those days (see p. 90).

The next and most important call of the day was Togg's (Toggnarelli's) ice cream parlour where we would have a ride in the lift which carried us to the entrance at a higher level. Once again half of the population of Bolton must have passed through its doors on a Saturday. The noise, the chatter, the laughter and the clinking of metal spoons on partially empty ice cream dishes would be savoured as you sipped your American cream soda. Time would pass with a happy satisfaction.

If only

When I was small
I had my picture taken with a ball
The picture man was Mr Fox.
He took it with a magic box.

For this picture of me I was brought to town
The picture man's price was half a crown.
So I had to smile and not to frown
It's not in colour, but a shade of brown.

I sat on the sideboard for all to see
Passed round relations when they came to tea

I was Mum and Dad's pride and joy.
Their one and only little boy.

As I am no longer small
In fact you could say rather tall
I still look at that picture now on the wall
And think of that little boy with a ball.

Can we try again Mr Fox
Take my picture with your magic box
Not however with a ball or balloon
This time make it a 'silver spoon'.

Bolton Town Hall, Victoria Square, 1963, showing a much quieter
pace of life.

Town Hall Tavern, behind Bolton Town Hall, it was demolished in 1925 and became part of the Civic Centre.

Mr Toggnarelli would be observed behind the counter in his black suit and fedora, giving help and assistance to his staff.

My wife Doreen told me that when she was fifteen years of age she worked part-time Saturdays and Sundays, 2.00 p.m. to 9.00 p.m. for 16s with certain freebies and that Mr Toggnarelli was an absolute gentleman and respected by one and all. Togg's was the in-scene – the Hard Rock Café of the day.

As all good things come to an end we would reluctantly have to leave to join the outside world. Our next goal was the Town Hall square and, even in those days, the challenge was, if the opportunity presented itself, to climb and sit on top of one of its magnificent stone lions. I only ever managed the challenge once and received many a backhander from an irate member of the public on previous attempts.

The Silver Vat public house, Bolton, also called the Four Horseshoes and the Lion's Paw, closed down in 1927 and the building became an extension of the Westminster Bank.

Newport Street was the heart of the town with the Commercial Hotel at one end and at the other the Wheatsheaf, this section being the main attractive part of the street.

We would window-shop down one side before crossing and returning down the other. If we needed to know the time of day and the Town Hall clock was obstructed from sight there was always the clock over Samuels the jewellers.

We would stand outside the UCP tripe shop viewing the contents of the window: cowheels, honeycomb and seam tripe with other revolting looking similarities and think 'Who eats such rubbish?' One day I was to find out – it was to be tripe for tea. Mother, Father and Aunty Wright soaked it in vinegar, sprinkled it with pepper and scoffed the lot. Myself under threat of death managed one piece, but after that no chance!

There was Hampson's confectioners, who at that time had a Silver Service café upstairs and close by Timpson's, my mother's favourite shoeshop where sometimes I would be bought a pair of black leather Oxford shoes which, on recollection, in those days were not cheap.

From Newport Street our Saturday adventure was approaching its climax as we would make our way to the aquarium and museum. The aquarium would be visited first and all its creatures studied and imitated – before running upstairs to the museum with all its treasures – on eventually leaving the museum a careful eye would be cast for any official attendants in the vicinity. If all was clear we would climb onto the stair rail and slide down to the bottom. A complete full circle of the town had quenched our energies, stimulated our minds and gave us the realisation that as Boltonians all this was ours, not forgetting that if we had three pennies it was a ride home on the train.

11

The Adult World

The war was over and I was almost a teenager. My next adventure was to prepare for a working life and introduction to the adult world with all its complexities. I started my first job in 1948 at the Croal Spinning Company, Deane, Bolton and this was a shock to the system. The working environment was very dirty, noisy, hot and dusty,with cotton fibres floating in the atmosphere which would irritate the eyes, nose and mouth. This was a spinning mill which in the

textile industry was known as the dirty end of the trade, meaning the hardest and dirtiest jobs with the poorest wages.

My father had wanted me to join him and become a motor mechanic, but Mother would not have it. She argued that the mill would provide a steady job now that the war had ended. On my first day Mother gave me a small scrubbing brush to take to work. This was to brush the cotton fibres off my clothing before coming home.

On entering a spinning mill you found that it had an unmistakable smell of its own – this was due to the natural oils in the cotton, the oil-soaked floor-boards, all combined with the very hot and humid atmosphere. The working environment was also con-taminated with a battering of noise, metal against metal, with hundreds of leather belts slapping against steel pulleys in the relentless driving of the machines. People would shout and wave their arms to attract

Croal Spinning Co, Bolton, 1972, spinners of fine mule yarns, showing the entrance to the mill yard and offices.

attention which is why the art of lip-reading naturally developed.

It was a dangerous place to work as many of the machines that the tenters ran were very poorly guarded and accidents were frequent. The Croal was a privately owned company, not part of any larger group, and produced very fine mule-spun yarns. As a new apprentice I did fall for some of the pranks played on me by my mentors – I already knew about the bucket of steam. But I did go to the engine house for a 'long stand' which lasted about thirty minutes and I also went to borrow a pair of 'six-inch sky hooks'. Every day was part of the learning curve.

My own boss, or to be correct 'overlooker' was Jack Higson who lived on Willows Lane, a very clever man who passed on all his knowledge to myself during my apprenticeship. I also remember him for his grin and a wry sense of humour. In my observations the textile industry was frowned on in general by society but to realise that in this part of the world is where it was born. It grew and developed here.

We had the engineers, the technicians and the know-how, also the right climate. We had a large available workforce, mainly of women who were glad to work even in adverse conditions for a regular income. There was not a great deal of job satisfaction at the end of the day. However, the driving force was the paypacket at the end of the week. Food had to be put on the table.

My workmate at the time and myself were often asked to work overtime in the evenings and Saturday mornings. Whatever the work was, the rate was ordinary time. This was a rule of the company, take it or leave it. One regular backbreaking job was picking string out of the cotton. We would go into large open bays piled high with cotton and by hand take armfuls and examine it for pieces of string which we would remove. Your eyes and nose would become full of fibres and the more you rubbed the more irritated they would become. Our success was measured by the amount of string that was found. When finished we would both look like snowmen.

The worst overtime job of all was the cleaning of the dust passages in the bowels of the mill. The passages themselves would be about five feet in height and five feet in width. These were accessed through a steel door at ground level. Our cleaning equipment consisted of a sweeping brush each, a hand torch, and a brass pump filled with DDT. After going through the door you stepped onto the floor of the passage which would be about twelve inches deep in cotton dust, short fibre, and seed. Our job was to sweep all this out, later to be put into bags, and at the same time brush the walls and ceiling clean. The brass pump with DDT was to spray the walls and ceiling to kill the hundreds of cockroaches that had made this place their home. As you can imagine it took many trips in and out of the passages to remove all this material. The main concern during these trips was that dying cockroaches would be falling from the ceiling onto you know who. After finishing the job your body would be crying out for a drink.

Our salvation was a fountain of life. This was in the form of a sink in the cardroom, with a solitary cold water tap. The sink itself was chipped and the décor surrounding it unpleasant but the water was straight from Iceland. It was cold and sparkling clear, even on the hottest of days. We would stand there, leaning on the wall, drinking pint after pint. This was our reward and made life bearable, not forgetting that the overtime had increased my wage to today's equivalent of £1.25 a week. This particular job was only carried out on a Saturday morning when the mill was stopped, and afterwards my workmate and myself would sometimes go to Chorlton's on Manchester Road to learn dancing. If only the girls had known where we had been and what had been dropping on us!

In those early days of my working life at the Croal Spinning Company I cannot remember any of the workforce, including the management, owning or using a car for travelling to work. The only transport we had at the mill was a wooden handcart which had two large wheels. I wished I had one pound for every time I pushed that cart up and down Deane Road. One day there was a great panic – a large component had broken and the mill was grinding to a halt! Did I know how to push a handcart? Of course, I replied (milk boy delivery experiences). I was told to get the cart and take the broken component to Angle Bank Welding Company for repair.

I pushed and rattled up Blackshaw Lane onto Deane Road, cut through Quebec Street up Peace Street onto Derby Street, down the full length of High Street to Lever Street and onto Angle Bank. On entering the workshop through a side door I was in an Aladdin's cave of broken rusty metal spread out on benches. The men were working like beavers, showers of sparks, flashing blue lights; they were always busy. The foreman and I went back outside and he looked at the job which I had brought. He explained that it was a big job and would take three to four hours to repair. I asked him where could I wait in the meantime. He suggested that if I had any money to go to the pictures for a couple of hours which would keep me out of their way. I told him I did not have any. He smiled at me, dug into his pocket and gave me sixpence. With this small fortune I made a quick departure and made my way to the Tivoli, being the nearest picture place.

I came out of the pictures in plenty of time and strolled back to Angle Bank. On arriving I found to my horror that the mill had been on the telephone to enquire about the job shortly after I had departed for the pictures. They had requested top priority and because of the urgency they were willing to pay any price, and for me to return as quickly as possible.

As I was at the pictures they had to send it back by taxi. I was now faced with a journey back to the mill, pushing an empty handcart and with questions to face. The following day the managing director, on his rounds of the mill, stopped me and asked had I enjoyed the film the previous day? He told me they were thinking of purchasing a works van for any future emergencies. This however never materialised: they still carried on with the image of Steptoe and Son and I was the horse!

A long-established tradition in the mills was at Christmas time when they had what was called a 'foot-in'. This would take place on the day that they finished for the holidays. The operatives (tenters) would decorate the area around their machines with streamers and decorations. They would prepare their spread for the afternoon, which would consist of sandwiches, sausage rolls, whist pies, mince pies and always a bottle of sherry.

At lunchtime all would leave the mill and invade the local pub. The time to return to work was often ignored and the rum and blacks kept flowing, even after threats from the management. When eventually returning back to the mill the foot-in would commence. All the machines would be left idle and the management would make threats of repercussions after the holidays. This was all in vain. The sherry and sausage rolls won every time.

As a young apprentice I was often bought a present by the women of the card room which was usually a fountain pen. One year, however, the card room had been split into two halves by a dispute between two of the women. I think one had been going out with the other's husband – it was war! As Christmas week approached, I was told by one half that I would get my pen as usual. The other half found out about this and told me they would give me a pen and also a wallet – 'real leather'. The first half then told me they had decided to up my present to a pen, a wallet, and also a watch! Would this ever end? I was rubbing my hands and counting chickens. This was to be the best Christmas ever. Alas, during Christmas week, the dispute was resolved by all concerned and I finished up with my usual fountain pen.

One of the dangers in a spinning mill was fire, which would occur quite often. You had the ingredients of a very flammable material combined with many sources of heat. The most common place was always the blowing room and the culprit was usually a small piece of bale iron, which had been carried through into the machines. We had a works fire-fighting team, which was chosen by the chief engineer. At the outbreak of a fire the team would spring into action and the battle would be fought. If the fire was getting out of control the fire brigade would be called. This would be done by the management rather reluctantly, as a considerable amount of damage would be caused by the water used.

When the fire was over the chief engineer would write down the names of all team members who had attended and they would receive an extra 5s (25p) in their wage.

On one of the walls in the blowing room was a small wooden cabinet which contained our secret weapon.

This was a very large pistol, which fired a large cartridge. In comparison it would be about six times larger than a modern twelve bore cartridge.

The cartridge contained a compressed white powder and, when fired at something solid, it would atomise into a fine cloud, which in turn would smother the fire.

At one particular fire that we were fighting, one of the team had taken possession of this pistol and was in the motion of selecting his target. At the same time the general manager had been taking a party of VIPs on a guided tour round the mill. Someone told him about the fire and he hastily made way to the scene with the VIPs following on.

He and his party appeared on the scene at the moment our marksman fired. The noise was thunderous and the recoil shoulder-breaking. The fired charge missed its mark, gave a glancing blow to the side of a machine, it then bounced off the side of a pillar and took a vertical path before exploding on the ceiling.

A large white cloud descended gently and covered one and all, and our party of VIPs were instantly turned into a party of irate 'flour graders'. Needless to say our secret weapon was confiscated and never seen again. I attended many fires over the years, some very serious but that one had given the greatest satisfaction!

Besides the working environment leaving a lot to be desired, sometimes being described as 'satanic', I found as a young man that the working hours were depressing. The working day was 7.30 a.m. start, 5.30 p.m. finish. I was expected to work two lunch hours a week, Wednesday and Friday, also two evenings and Saturday morning. I know overtime was take it or leave it but from the point-of-view of keeping your job it was not wise to leave it.

My Mother and Father had always drummed into me that you go to work to put a wage on the table, that in turn puts food on the table, so therefore if you do not work you do not eat. The day before I had started my first job, my Father gave me advice which I have never forgotten. When I drew my wage at the end of the week, it had to be given to my Mother who in turn would give me my spending money. As I was now entering the adult world I would see that men spent their money on various pastimes. Drink was one of these pastimes but as I was too young this did not concern me. Women were another but as I was just a boy any thoughts should be left to much later in life. Then there was gambling and the evil of horseracing. After working all week to take my hard-earned money, which was hard-earned, and gamble it on a horse was stupidity. 'It is like this, Arnold, if there are ten horses in a race you have to pick the winner and put your money on it. The bookmaker has the other nine horses so who is stupid?' I had to agree that his logic was more than sound.

As my apprenticeship was nearing its end at the Croal Spinning Company, the management advised me to begin looking for a new position for the next step forward, which I did with a feeling of uncertainty. If there had been a suitable vacancy I would have liked to have stayed but, alas, no. It may seem strange to say that even with the dirt and noise a mill becomes a way of life and a place of security for the generations that have trodden the oil-soaked floorboards.